Contents

JN021375

リスニング音声は英俊社ウェブサイト「リスもん」から再生できます。

再生の際は右のコードを入力してください。　96457823

スマホは
こちら

https://book.eisyun.jp/products/listening/index/

は　し　が　き

　本書は，大阪府公立高等学校の一般入学者選抜における，英語Ｃ問題の対策問題集です。

　大阪府公立高等学校一般入学者選抜では，平成 28 年度入試から，英語・数学・国語について，3 種類の学力検査問題が作成されており，その中で難易度が最も高い問題がＣ問題です。

　また，平成 29 年度入試からは，英語Ｃ問題について，「『実践的に使える』英語教育への転換に向けた改革」が実施されています。

　大阪府教育委員会によって公表された，その改革の主要なポイントは次の通りです。

1．「聞く・書く」力をより試す問題に

　「読む・聞く・書く・話す」の 4 技能のうち，「聞く（リスニング）」・「書く（ライティング）」の配点が大きく増加し，「話す」以外の 3 技能を均等化します。

　「聞く（リスニング）」は，従来の約 20 ％から約 33 ％に，「書く（ライティング）」は，従来の約 8 ％から約 20 ％に増加し，「聞く・書く」を合わせて 50 ％を超えることになります。

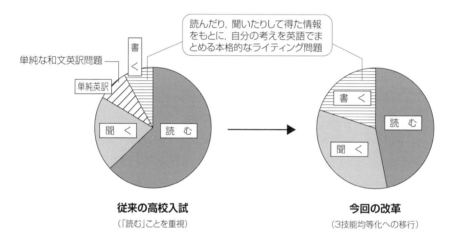

2．より高度な「読む」力を求める

　従来の試験と比較し，英文の量は選択肢を含め大きく増加し，1 分間に読まなくてはならない語数は 96 語程度です。これは従来の語数に比べて 2.7 倍にもなります。

3．問題文はすべて英語

　指示文を含め，問題文はすべて英語で構成されます。（日本語は単語の注釈のみに使用されます。）

左記のような観点から作成される検査問題に対しては，既存の問題集では十分な準備ができないと思われることから，本書が編集されました。

　文法項目・読解演習・英作文・リスニングの出題分野ごとに，想定される難易度・出題形式の問題を掲載しています。本書を通して，新傾向の検査問題に対応できる力を身につけてください。

　また，入試本番の試験形式での演習として，「**大阪府公立高等学校 一般 予想テスト**」が英俊社から秋に発行されます。英語Ｃ問題の改革に沿ったテストも収録していますので，直前の対策として活用されることをお勧めします。

※Ｃ問題を出題する高等学校の一覧など最新の入試情報については，大阪府教育委員会のホームページでご確認ください。

Chapter 1 *Grammar*

§1. 誤文訂正

● There are four underlined words or phrases in the sentences below. Choose the one word or phrase which is wrong.

(1)　We will have to stay at a hotel if it will rain tomorrow. (　　)

　　ア　will　　イ　stay at　　ウ　if　　エ　will rain

(2)　Are there any interesting news in today's newspaper? (　　)

　　ア　Are　　イ　any　　ウ　interesting　　エ　today's

(3)　A :　I don't like speaking in front of people.

　　　B :　I don't like it, too. I feel nervous. (　　)

　　ア　speaking　　イ　front　　ウ　too　　エ　feel

(4)　My baby is sleeping in the next room. Don't noisy. (　　)

　　ア　is sleeping　　イ　in　　ウ　the next room　　エ　Don't noisy

(5)　She has been sick for yesterday. (　　)

　　ア　has　　イ　been　　ウ　sick　　エ　for

(6)　Excuse me, may I have two glasses of waters? (　　)

　　ア　Excuse me　　イ　may I　　ウ　two glasses　　エ　of waters

(7)　I buy these shoes at that shop yesterday. (　　)

　　ア　buy　　イ　these　　ウ　at　　エ　that

(8)　Let's go to the restaurant and drink hot something, shall we? (　　)

　　ア　go to　　イ　drink　　ウ　hot something　　エ　shall we

(9)　One of my friends are going to buy a new car. (　　)

　　ア　One of　　イ　friends　　ウ　are　　エ　buy

(10)　Tom will be surprising to know that. (　　)

　　ア　will　　イ　be　　ウ　surprising　　エ　to know

(11)　How much cars were there in the street yesterday morning? (　　)

　　ア　How much　　イ　were there　　ウ　in the street　　エ　yesterday morning

(12)　Reading English books are very difficult for me. (　　)

　　ア　Reading　　イ　are　　ウ　very difficult　　エ　for me

(13)　I went to America last summer. While my stay in New York, I visited the Statue of Liberty. (　　)

　　ア　went　　イ　While　　ウ　my　　エ　visited

(14) When she <u>drives</u> a car, Kathy is <u>more</u> <u>carefully</u> than <u>her sister</u>. (　　　)

　　ア　drives　　イ　more　　ウ　carefully　　エ　her sister

(15) Look <u>at</u> the man <u>in a cap</u> and the dog <u>who</u> are running <u>over there</u>. (　　　)

　　ア　at　　イ　in a cap　　ウ　who　　エ　over there

(16) <u>The boy</u> <u>standing</u> <u>over there</u> is a friend <u>of me</u>. (　　　)

　　ア　The boy　　イ　standing　　ウ　over there　　エ　of me

(17) Leo <u>likes</u> <u>history</u> <u>better</u> of <u>all the</u> subjects. (　　　)

　　ア　likes　　イ　history　　ウ　better　　エ　all the

(18) He <u>knows</u> <u>what</u> he will have to spend <u>a lot of</u> <u>money</u> on it. (　　　)

　　ア　knows　　イ　what　　ウ　a lot of　　エ　money

(19) The picture of <u>a</u> woman <u>drawing</u> <u>by</u> Ken was <u>very</u> beautiful. (　　　)

　　ア　a　　イ　drawing　　ウ　by　　エ　very

(20) Mr. and Mrs. Harrison <u>are</u> <u>Americans</u> who <u>has moved</u> to Japan <u>more than</u> fifteen years ago. (　　　)

　　ア　are　　イ　Americans　　ウ　has moved　　エ　more than

(21) That student <u>fell</u> <u>asleep</u> <u>just</u> after <u>get</u> home. (　　　)

　　ア　fell　　イ　asleep　　ウ　just　　エ　get

(22) Cathy <u>studies</u> Japanese and Chinese. The books she <u>read</u> yesterday <u>was written</u> <u>in</u> Chinese. (　　　)

　　ア　studies　　イ　read　　ウ　was written　　エ　in

(23) Yuki went <u>shopping</u> last Sunday. She saw <u>one of</u> her <u>classmates</u>, so she stopped <u>talking</u> with her. (　　　)

　　ア　shopping　　イ　one of　　ウ　classmates　　エ　talking

(24) Mary <u>wants</u> Tom <u>join</u> the party <u>with</u> <u>her</u> this evening. (　　　)

　　ア　wants　　イ　join　　ウ　with　　エ　her

(25) This is the watch <u>giving</u> <u>to</u> me <u>by</u> my grandfather <u>on</u> Christmas. (　　　)

　　ア　giving　　イ　to　　ウ　by　　エ　on

(26) <u>At</u> school I <u>enjoy</u> <u>to play</u> with <u>my friends</u>. (　　　)

　　ア　At　　イ　enjoy　　ウ　to play　　エ　my friends

(27) I <u>have wanted</u> to <u>go to abroad</u> to study English since I was little. Finally, I am going <u>to visit England</u> next year. I hope <u>to make</u> many friends there. (　　　)

　　ア　have wanted　　イ　go to abroad　　ウ　to visit England　　エ　to make

(28) Japanese food <u>loved</u> by many people in the world and <u>there are</u> a lot of Japanese restaurants. Even Japanese tourists look forward <u>to eating</u> their favorite food while <u>they are traveling</u>. (　　　)

　　ア　loved　　イ　there are　　ウ　to eating　　エ　they are traveling

§2．英文完成

● Choose the one word or phrase that best completes the sentence.

(1) My friend sometimes （　　　） breakfast on Sunday.

　　ア　cook　　イ　cooks　　ウ　cooking　　エ　is cooked

(2) Judy and Ken （　　　） studying in the room now.

　　ア　is　　イ　was　　ウ　are　　エ　were

(3) You may （　　　） now.

　　ア　go　　イ　went　　ウ　going　　エ　gone

(4) English is the language （　　　） all over the world.

　　ア　speak　　イ　spoke　　ウ　spoken　　エ　speaking

(5) Do you know the woman （　　　） there?

　　ア　running　　イ　ran　　ウ　run　　エ　is run

(6) Sam （　　　） to hear the news.

　　ア　surprised　　イ　was surprising　　ウ　were surprised　　エ　was surprised

(7) （　　　） you tell me the way to Aikawa Station?

　　ア　Could　　イ　Were　　ウ　Have　　エ　When

(8) Have you （　　　） your homework yet?

　　ア　did　　イ　do　　ウ　done　　エ　does

(9) My mother （　　　） a movie when I came home.

　　ア　watches　　イ　watched　　ウ　has watched　　エ　was watching

(10) Thank you （　　　） helping me.

　　ア　at　　イ　for　　ウ　with　　エ　in

(11) You should go home （　　　） it rains.

　　ア　but　　イ　before　　ウ　or　　エ　that

(12) Summer is my favorite season （　　　） I can swim in the sea.

　　ア　if　　イ　or　　ウ　but　　エ　because

(13) How （　　　） is it from your home to the airport?

　　ア　long　　イ　far　　ウ　old　　エ　often

(14) My children sometimes go to school （　　　） train.

　　ア　by　　イ　for　　ウ　at　　エ　over

(15) I will write this letter （　　　） English.

　　ア　in　　イ　by　　ウ　with　　エ　on

(16) We go to school （　　　） Monday to Saturday.

　　ア　in　　イ　from　　ウ　on　　エ　of

(17) ( ) did you eat for breakfast?

ア Who 　イ Why 　ウ Where 　エ What

(18) You can ski ( ) than me.

ア good 　イ well 　ウ better 　エ best

(19) Please look at ( ) in the mirror.

ア I 　イ your 　ウ yourself 　エ yours

(20) There are many movies ( ) children like.

ア what 　イ which 　ウ who 　エ whose

(21) ( ) English is difficult for me.

ア Speaking 　イ Spoke 　ウ That speak 　エ Speaking of

(22) ( ) quiet in this room.

ア Do 　イ Don't 　ウ Be 　エ Being

(23) Would you like ( ) coffee?

ア few 　イ some 　ウ little 　エ no

(24) My sister gets up ( ) in my family.

ア faster 　イ the fastest 　ウ earlier 　エ the earliest

(25) I want to go to Australia ( ) English.

ア study 　イ studies 　ウ studied 　エ to study

(26) A : Mom, could you pass me the salt?

　　B : Oh, Julia. Be careful. Taking ( ) is not good for your health.

ア too much salt 　イ too much salts 　ウ too many salt 　エ too many salts

(27) A : What do you want to do in the future?

　　B : I like traveling, so I would like to visit ( ) in the world.

ア every country 　イ to every country 　ウ every countries 　エ to every countries

(28) A : Excuse me. Do you know ( )?

　　B : No, I'm sorry. I'm not from around here.

ア where is the post office 　イ where the post office is 　ウ where does the post office

エ where does the post office is

(29) The cat is ( ) all my family.

ア called Kitty 　イ calling Kitty 　ウ called Kitty to 　エ called Kitty by

(30) A : You don't know who discovered America, do you?

　　B : ( ). I'm not good at history.

ア Yes, I don't 　イ Yes, I do 　ウ No, I do 　エ No, I don't

(31) A : The flowers in the garden ( ). You must water them.

　　B : I'll do it right now.

ア are dying 　イ are dead 　ウ are died 　エ have died

§3. 実践問題

● Choose the phrase that best completes each sentence below.

(1) The woman asked me (　　　).

ア　how buy the ticket to 　　イ　to how buy the ticket

ウ　how to buy the ticket 　　エ　to the ticket buy how

(2) I wish (　　　).

ア　I could to go the party 　　イ　could I go to the party

ウ　I could go to the party 　　エ　could I go the party to

(3) Sugar is (　　　).

ア　sweet dishes used to make 　　イ　used to make dishes sweet

ウ　sweet used to make dishes 　　エ　used make dishes to sweet

(4) That hat was (　　　).

ア　not as this one as expensive 　　イ　as expensive not as this one

ウ　not as expensive as this one 　　エ　as not expensive as this one

(5) Yuki's parents (　　　).

ア　study to often tell her hard 　　イ　often tell hard study to her

ウ　study often hard tell her to 　　エ　often tell her to study hard

(6) Will you (　　　)?

ア　carry my bags help me 　　イ　help my bags me carry

ウ　carry me help my bags 　　エ　help me carry my bags

(7) What would you (　　　)?

ア　had much money if you do 　　イ　do if you had much money

ウ　had if you do much money 　　エ　do much money if you had

(8) The girl (　　　) is my sister.

ア　who is doing her homework 　　イ　is doing her homework who

ウ　who is her homework doing 　　エ　is doing who her homework

(9) The math problem (　　　).

ア　was to me too difficult for solve 　　イ　to solve too difficult was for me

ウ　was too difficult for me to solve 　　エ　to me was too difficult for solve

(10) I'm going to give my son (　　　).

ア　the guitar that my uncle gave me 　　イ　that my uncle gave me the guitar

ウ　the guitar my uncle gave me that 　　エ　that the guitar my uncle gave me

(11) My parents (　　　) in high school.

ア　let me study abroad when I was 　　イ　study me abroad when I was let

ウ　let me abroad when I was study 　　エ　study abroad when I was let me

(12) (　　　　) built about twenty years ago.

　　ア　There was the standing house over　　イ　The house standing over there was

　　ウ　There was the house over standing　　エ　The standing over there house was

(13)　Plastic bags (　　　) many serious problems to animals.

　　ア　into the ocean throw people cause　　イ　people throw into the ocean cause

　　ウ　into cause people throw the ocean　　エ　people cause throw into the ocean

(14)　Osaka is (　　　) from different countries.

　　ア　visited a city by many people　　イ　a city visited by many people

　　ウ　visited many people by a city　　エ　a city many people visited by

(15)　Our teacher said (　　　) try to understand other people's feelings.

　　ア　to us for necessary it was really　　イ　it was necessary to us really for

　　ウ　to us really necessary for it was　　エ　it was really necessary for us to

(16)　Those science textbooks were so difficult (　　　).

　　ア　them understand that I couldn't　　イ　that I couldn't understand them

　　ウ　them I couldn't understand that　　エ　that couldn't I understand them

(17)　Can you tell me (　　　) for the dinner party?

　　ア　what kind of clothes I should wear　　イ　I should wear kind of what clothes

　　ウ　what clothes kind of should I wear　　エ　I wear what kind of clothes should

(18)　I (　　　) the welcome party for Ms. Smith.

　　ア　wanted to join everyone in the team　　イ　join everyone in the team to wanted

　　ウ　wanted everyone in the team to join　　エ　join wanted everyone in the team to

(19)　The restaurant (　　　) a different town yesterday.

　　ア　moved many years ago which opened to

　　イ　which opened many years ago moved to

　　ウ　moved to which opened many years ago

　　エ　which moved many years ago opened to

(20)　Mari (　　　) a book.

　　ア　was happy that her uncle bought her　　イ　that was happy her uncle bought her

　　ウ　was happy her uncle bought that her　　エ　that her uncle was happy bought her

(21)　My grandmother has been (　　　) in the park for a year.

　　ア　growing the plants to giving water　　イ　giving the plants water to growing

　　ウ　growing the plants giving water to　　エ　giving water to the plants growing

(22)　Kyoko wanted to know (　　　) dish.

　　ア　how much sugar to cook that she needed

　　イ　that how much sugar she needed to cook

　　ウ　how much sugar she needed to cook that

　　エ　that she needed to cook how much sugar

Chapter2 *Reading*

§1. 図表を含む問題

1 Read the passage and choose the answer which best completes each sentence (1) and (2).

Young people from age 18 to 24 were asked some questions about volunteer work and the graph shows their answers. ☐A☐ If you look at the graph, you can see information about the rate of young people who are now doing, have done, or have never done volunteer work in each country.

In the U.S., about 20% of young people are doing volunteer work now, but about 40% of them have never done it. ☐B☐ In Korea and Japan, less than 10% of young people are doing volunteer work now. However, more young people in Korea have done volunteer work than young people in Japan. ☐C☐ In Japan, France, and Korea, more than 50% of young people have never done volunteer work before, and among ①them Japan has the largest number of people who have never done volunteer work.

Some people think volunteer work is good for young people because they can do something good for other people through volunteer work. ☐D☐ So, what do you think about doing volunteer work?

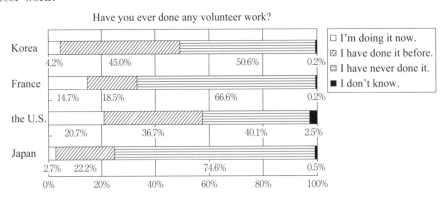

Have you ever done any volunteer work?

Legend:
□ I'm doing it now.
☑ I have done it before.
⊟ I have never done it.
■ I don't know.

Korea: 4.2% | 45.0% | 50.6% | 0.2%
France: 14.7% | 18.5% | 66.6% | 0.2%
the U.S.: 20.7% | 36.7% | 40.1% | 2.5%
Japan: 2.7% | 22.2% | 74.6% | 0.5%

(1) The sentence "However, other people think young people do not have to do it because they are busy with studying and club activities." should be put in (　　)

ア ☐A☐.　イ ☐B☐.　ウ ☐C☐.　エ ☐D☐.

(2) The word ① them refers to （　　　）

ア the U.S. and Korea.

イ Japan, France, and Korea.

ウ Japan and France.

エ the U.S. and Japan.

2 Read the passage and choose the answer which best completes each sentence (1) and (2).

What do you do on holidays? ☐A☐ This graph shows what young people in Japan and Brazil do on holidays. ☐B☐ Young Japanese people like spending time with friends. It is the most popular thing that they do on holidays. On the other hand, in Brazil, spending time with family is the most popular activity. ☐C☐ In Japan shopping is

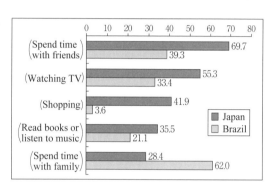

more popular than reading books or listening to music. But in Brazil ① it is not. Only a small percentage of young people there go shopping on holidays. ☐D☐ In both countries watching TV is more popular than shopping.

(注) graph グラフ　Brazil ブラジル　activity 活動　percentage 割合

(1) The sentence "More than 60% of young people there do that." should be put in （　　　）

ア ☐A☐.　イ ☐B☐.　ウ ☐C☐.　エ ☐D☐.

(2) The word ① it refers to （　　　）

ア shopping.

イ reading books or listening to music.

ウ watching TV.

エ spending time with friends.

3 Read the passage and choose the answer which best completes each sentence (1) and (2).

What makes the earth warmer? Maybe you know the answer. Too much CO_2. China produces the most CO_2 in the world. ☐A☐ The United States comes second. How about Japan? The graph shows that Japan also produces a lot of CO_2. Every country should try harder to reduce it. ☐B☐ We should do something for our earth.

What should we do? I have two ideas. ☐C☐ Most of our energy comes from sources that produce a lot of CO_2. Turn off the TV when you are not watching it. Using a bus or a train is better than using a car. Second, we should try to save the forests. Trees are very important. They reduce CO_2 in the air because they need ①it to grow. But many trees are cut down to make paper. Just remember that we use a lot of paper every day. Don't throw away notebooks you can still use. ☐D☐ Use paper bags again and again. These are small things, but if everyone works together, we can help to save the earth.

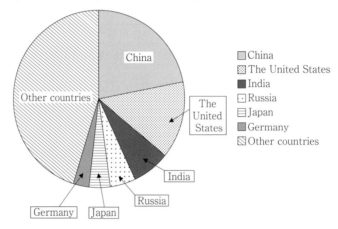

※This graph was issued in 2022.

（注） sources　資源

(1) The sentence "First, we should stop using too much energy." should be put in （　　　）
ア ☐A☐ .　　イ ☐B☐ .　　ウ ☐C☐ .　　エ ☐D☐ .

(2) The word ①it refers to （　　　）
ア　the tree.
イ　CO_2.
ウ　the air.
エ　the paper.

4　Read the passage and choose the answer which best completes each sentence (1) and (2).

Do you have breakfast every morning?　There are some people who don't like to eat breakfast and start the day without it.　But breakfast is very important.　When you eat breakfast, your body will be warm.　Your sleeping brain will be active, too.　A

Look at the graph.　Breakfast has some influence on the health of your body.　More than 50% of the people who eat breakfast every day say, "I feel well."　And about 65% of the people who skip breakfast three days or more in a week say, "I don't feel well."　B

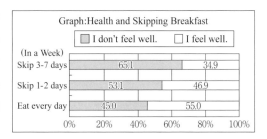

Breakfast also has ① some influence on the health of your mind.　For example, when something bad happens, breakfast skippers will be upset or angry more often than people who eat breakfast.　It is sometimes difficult for those breakfast skippers to think very carefully about one thing for a long time.　C

If you eat breakfast, you need time for it.　What should we do to have time in the morning?　The first thing you should do is to get up early.　And to get up early, you should stop sitting in front of the TV or a computer and go to bed early.　To live a regular life makes regular eating habits.　And the health of your mind and body comes from your regular eating habits. D　Did you have breakfast this morning?

(注)　brain　脳　　active　活発な　　influence　影響　　health　健康
　　　skip breakfast　朝食を抜く　　regular　規則的な

(1)　The sentence "The health of your mind is kept by eating breakfast." should be put in

（　　　）

ア　A .　　イ　B .　　ウ　C .　　エ　D .

(2)　The words ① some influence on the health of your mind mean that （　　　）
　ア　bad things will always happen to breakfast skippers.
　イ　breakfast skippers sometimes can't be careful when they have to think.
　ウ　breakfast skippers will go to bed late and can't get up early.
　エ　breakfast skippers like to sit in front of the TV or a computer.

5 Read the passage and choose the answer which best completes sentence (1), and choose the answer which best completes each blank ① and ②.

    A survey about the average number of books junior high school and high school students read in May, from 2009 to 2017 in Japan was done. The table shows its results. ☐A☐ About 3,000 junior high school students and about 3,600 high school students responded. ☐B☐ Every year, junior high school students read more books than high school students. Junior high school students read the most books in 2017 and high school students in 2010. ☐C☐ On the other hand, junior high school students read the fewest books in 2009 and 2011. ☐D☐ And high school students read [①   ]. Let's look at the total average number of books that junior high school students and high school students read. [②   ]. The second largest number is 6.0 in 2017.

    （注）survey 調査　average 平均の　table 表　result 結果　on the other hand 一方で

【Table】

The average numbers of the answer to the question: "How many books did you read in May?"									
student＼year	2009	2010	2011	2012	2013	2014	2015	2016	2017
Junior high school students	3.7	4.2	3.7	4.2	4.1	3.9	4.0	4.2	4.5
High school students	1.7	1.9	1.8	1.6	1.7	1.6	1.5	1.4	1.5

（公益社団法人　全国学校図書館協議会「第63回学校読書調査」(2017年) により作成）

(1) The sentence "The question was 'How many books did you read in May?'" should be put in (　　　)

ア ☐A☐.　イ ☐B☐.　ウ ☐C☐.　エ ☐D☐.

(2) ① ア　the most books in 2011   (　　　)

      イ　the most books in 2016

      ウ　the fewest books in 2016

      エ　the fewest books in 2017

(3) ② ア　The largest number is 6.1 in 2010   (　　　)

      イ　The largest number is 6.2 in 2010

      ウ　The smallest number is 5.4 in 2010

      エ　The smallest number is 5.5 in 2011

6　Read the passage and choose the answer which best completes each blank ①～③.

In 2019, a Japanese company did a survey.　About 5,600 people over 19 years old answered questions on the Internet.　To the question "Do you do exercise or sports regularly?", about one-third of the people who joined the survey said yes.　They chose one or more activities to the question, "What activities do you regularly do?"　The table shows seven popular choices and the percentage of people who chose them.　The table only shows four groups: men and women who were 20-29 years old, and men and women who were 50-59 years old.

We see that 　①　 placed first or second in all four groups.　However, we also found some differences in regular activities for each group.　For example, bodily exercises was chosen by only 5.8 percent of men who were 20-29 years old, but 37.8 percent of women who were 50-59 years old chose it.　Of the seven choices, 　②　 placed fourth among women who were 20-29 years old, but it was in the lowest place among men who were 50-59 years old.　There is another thing we can learn from this table.　The percentage of people who chose 　③　 varied most greatly among the four groups.　The largest percentage difference is over 50.

（注）　survey　アンケート調査　　exercise　運動　　regularly　定期的に　　table　表

　　　　percentage　割合　　place　～位になる　　vary　異なる　　greatly　非常に

【Table】

activities ＼ group	20-29 (men)	20-29 (women)	50-59 (men)	50-59 (women)
Walking（ウォーキング）	34.2%	65.7%	63.8%	51.1%
Running（ランニング）	62.6%	41.2%	28.9%	7.4%
Bodily exercises（体操）	5.8%	25.5%	13.8%	37.8%
Golf（ゴルフ）	9.7%	1.0%	19.1%	3.7%
Swimming（水泳）	11.6%	9.8%	6.6%	9.6%
Cycling（サイクリング）	9.7%	6.9%	9.9%	3.7%
Climbing mountains（登山）	12.3%	6.9%	8.6%	4.4%

What activities do you regularly do?

（明治安田生命「『健康』に関するアンケート調査」（2019 年）により作成）

(1)　①　ア　Walking　　　　　　　　　　　　　　　（　　　）

　　　イ　Running

　　　ウ　Bodily exercises

　　　エ　Swimming

(2) ② ア Golf   (   )

      イ Swimming

      ウ Cycling

      エ Climbing Mountains

(3) ③ ア Walking   (   )

      イ Running

      ウ Bodily exercises

      エ Golf

§2．短い英文を読む問題①

1 Read the passage and choose the answer which best completes each sentence (1)～(5).

Communication means sending a thought from one person to another or from one place to another. The easiest way is to talk. When you say something, your friend hears you and understands ① <u>your meaning</u>. The only problem is this: how do you tell things to your friend when she or he is in a different place?

Well, one way is just to visit your friend. But sometimes that is difficult. For example, if your friend lives very far away, you may need to fly in an airplane to get to your friend in one day. In the old days, people sent messages over long way with runners. You would tell your thought to the runner, and the runner would run or travel to your friend and tell her or him. This was the only way to communicate through most of human history. But this way of communication was very slow and hard.

Sometimes, people would use other ways of communication. In Africa, people would use music to send thoughts. One person could hit a drum and another person could hear it and understand the meaning. For example, maybe hitting a drum three times, again and again, would mean "we have found food."

In North America, people used to send thoughts with smoke. They would make a fire, and change the smoke rising from the fire. Someone far away could see the smoke in the air and understand the meaning. For example, maybe two big balls of smoke and one small one, again and again, could mean "send help."

Smoke and drums were useful, but messages could only go a short way using these ways. Today, by new machines and ideas for communication we can send our thoughts in ways that are much faster and easier than before.

(注)　thought　考え　　drum　太鼓　　smoke　煙　　rising (rise)　上がる　　machine　機械

(1)　This story is about （　　　）

　　ア　sending messages to others.　　　イ　why we need to communicate.

　　ウ　drums in Africa and North America.　　　エ　using smoke for sending messages.

(2)　The writer says that （　　　）

　　ア　communication is writing a letter to person.

　　イ　communication is the way an idea is passed from person to person.

　　ウ　communication is something that humans began to do a few years ago.

　　エ　communication is getting ideas from someone.

(3) In this situation, the words ①<u>your meaning</u> mean (　　　)

　　ア　what is difficult to tell.　　イ　the easiest way of talking.

　　ウ　what you want to tell your friend.　　エ　what your friend hears.

(4) The writer gives the example that hitting a drum three times means that (　　　)

　　ア　we have found food.　　イ　we will start to dance.　　ウ　we need to make a fire.

　　エ　we need help.

(5) People used smoke to communicate (　　　)

　　ア　in South Africa.　　イ　in South America.　　ウ　in North America.

　　エ　all over the world.

2　Read the passage and choose the answer which best completes each sentence (1)〜(5).

　　The Internet is useful when you are looking for information. You do not have to go to a library to find many different things. If you have a computer with the Internet, you have your own library. You can also find out about schools all over the world. One of my American friends living in Japan used the Internet and chose a school to go. He did not have to go back to America to visit many different schools. More than three hundred schools in Japan are on the Internet. If you want to know when to take a test or how much to pay, it's very easy to find out such information on the Internet.

　　You can use the Internet to send and to receive letters. I received a letter from a friend in America. He wanted to know about something. I answered him on the Internet, too. If we use ①<u>regular letters</u>, we will need about two weeks. But using the Internet helped us, and it took only three days to finish writing letters to each other.

　　You can also buy many things on the Internet. You don't have to go to different stores to decide what to buy. If you have something that you want to sell, you can use the Internet to sell it. You can be a business person. The Internet is used in schools, too. In many countries, the Internet gives classes to the children who live very far from schools. Having a computer at home is very useful, isn't it?

　　If the Internet can give you lessons, you may think that schools are not necessary any more. But is it true? If you don't go shopping in stores, and if you don't go to school to play with your friends, it is easy for you to become a person who can talk only on the computer and you will lose human emotions. In many countries, there are a lot of people with Internet

Syndrome. Schools will be necessary, because you learn not only your subjects but also human relations at school. You need to learn how to use the Internet, but learning to use it wisely is also important.

（注） emotion 感情　syndrome シンドローム, 症候群　relation 関係　wisely 賢く

(1)　On the Internet, （　　　）

　　ア　we can borrow books.

　　イ　we can make a real library.

　　ウ　we can get some information about schools.

　　エ　we can study anything without going to school.

(2)　A good point of sending and receiving letters on the Internet is （　　　）

　　ア　that we can send messages faster.

　　イ　that we can practice typing keyboard.

　　ウ　that we don't have to go to a post office.

　　エ　that e-mails can show our emotions better.

(3)　In this situation, the words ① regular letters mean （　　　）

　　ア　messages you write on paper　　イ　messages you send very often

　　ウ　messages you send by ship　　エ　messages you never write

(4)　The Internet is useful in schools （　　　）

　　ア　because students can become a business person.

　　イ　because students don't have to go to many stores to decide what to buy.

　　ウ　because students can buy many things on the Internet.

　　エ　because students can take lessons at home.

(5)　The writer says that schools will be necessary （　　　）

　　ア　because we cannot do anything without schools.

　　イ　because we cannot learn human relations without schools.

　　ウ　because we cannot learn how to use the Internet without schools.

　　エ　because we cannot have Internet Syndrome without schools.

3　Read the passage and choose the answer which best completes each sentence (1)〜(5).

　　In Japan, they are called *mahobin*. In English, they are called vacuum flasks. Almost every student has one. But do you know anything about these handy bottles?

　　The vacuum flask was invented by Sir James Dewar, a British scientist, in 1892. The first company to make lots of vacuum flasks for sale in shops was the German company Thermos Gmbh. It started making them in 1904. Since then, millions of Thermos flasks have been sold and they are so popular that people now call any kind of vacuum flask a "thermos" in most countries around the world.

　　Thermos flasks can be made of metal, glass or plastic. They are basically two bottles, one inside the other. There is no air in the small space between the two bottles — this is called a "① vacuum" in English. This protects the drink inside from the heat or cold of the air around it. They are very convenient, strong and light, so you can carry them anywhere. A normal vacuum flask will keep a drink cool for up to 24 hours or warm for up to 8 hours.

(1)　The first vacuum flask was made (　　　)

　　ア　more than a century ago.　　イ　in 1904.　　ウ　in Germany.

　　エ　for about 24 hours.

(2)　We use the name "thermos" for a vacuum flask (　　　)

　　ア　because it is easier to say thermos than vacuum.

　　イ　because the first one was made by the Thermos company.

　　ウ　because Thermos flasks are so popular around the world.

　　エ　because it was invented by Mr. James Thermos.

(3)　In this situation, the word ① vacuum means (　　　)

　　ア　no air.　　イ　no space.　　ウ　a bottle.　　エ　a thermos.

(4)　Thermos flasks can be carried anywhere (　　　)

　　ア　because they are small and light.　　イ　because they are strong and light.

　　ウ　because they are small and strong.　　エ　because they are warm and light.

(5)　The true sentence for this passage is (　　　)

　　ア　"no thermos flasks are sold in Japan."

　　イ　"thermos flasks can be made of wood."

　　ウ　"the thermos flask was invented in Japan in 1892."

　　エ　"thermos flasks can keep drinks cold for 24 hours."

4 Read the passage and choose the answer which best completes each blank in ①～③, and answer the question (4).

　　Betty is a student. She comes from Brazil. She is now staying with Sachiko's family. About two months ago she came to Japan to learn Japanese. Betty and Sachiko ___①___ .

　　Yesterday Mr. Sato said to the students, "Well, we are happy to have a nice student like Betty in this class. Now, what do you think about your life in Japan, Betty?"

　　Betty stood up and said, "When I first arrived, everything was new to me. Even now so many things look different. We often ___②___ , but you don't. In Brazil, Christmas comes in summer, but it comes in winter in Japan. At first I wasn't able to speak Japanese well. Now I'm studying it very hard. Sachiko helps me with my work. Other people are very kind to me, too. Now ___③___ ." Sachiko was glad to hear that.

　（注）　Brazil　ブラジル

(1)　①　ア　go to different schools　　　　　　　　　（　　）
　　　　イ　are in the same class
　　　　ウ　want to spend the time at the same school
　　　　エ　want to go to the same school

(2)　②　ア　take off our shoes in the house in our country　（　　）
　　　　イ　wear our shoes in the house in our country
　　　　ウ　have a Christmas party in our country
　　　　エ　have Christmas in winter in our country

(3)　③　ア　I'll miss Christmas in Brazil　　　　　　　（　　）
　　　　イ　I want to wear my shoes in the house
　　　　ウ　I'm enjoying my life here very much
　　　　エ　I want to go back to my country soon

(4)　What is the best title of this passage?　（　　　　）
　　ア　Japanese is Difficult
　　イ　The Life of Mr. Sato
　　ウ　Christmas in Brazil
　　エ　Homestay in Japan

5 Read the passage and choose the answer which best completes each blank in ①〜③, and answer the question (4).

Today about six billion people living on the earth use about 7,000 different languages. Some languages have many speakers. Chinese is one such language. About 900 million people speak a variety of Chinese. Other languages ［ ① ］. Eyak, a language in North America, has only one speaker.

The value of a language is not the number of speakers. All languages are important. Each language is the heart of its speaker.

Even in a single country people use many languages. Take India, for example. As you know, India is famous for its curry, but the taste of curry changes every 25 kilometers. This is also true of languages in India. If you travel 50 kilometers, you will ［ ② ］. Indians speak about 350 languages in total. Among them eighteen languages are official languages. So you can hear at least eighteen languages on TV or radio.

What about Japan? Some people say, "We ［ ③ ］." But this is not so. In Hokkaido, some people speak Ainu. Now about 1.6 million foreigners live in Japan. They come from 50 different countries.

Foreign languages are in our everyday life too. In Osaka, people can hear 14 different languages on a radio station. In big cities like Tokyo, we see some public signs in more than one language. So we can call some towns in Japan 'multilingual' communities.

（注）　billion　10億　　a variety of　様々な　　Eyak　イーヤク語(アメリカ先住民の一言語)
value　価値　　single　たった１つの　　taste　味　　in total　全体で
official language　公用語　　at least　少なくとも　　Ainu　アイヌ語　　public sign　標識

(1) ①　ア　have very few speakers　　　　　　　　　　（　　　）
　　　　イ　have a lot of speakers
　　　　ウ　have more speakers than Chinese
　　　　エ　have as many speakers as Chinese

(2) ②　ア　find a different kind of curry　　　　　　　　（　　　）
　　　　イ　hear a different language
　　　　ウ　hear eighteen languages
　　　　エ　watch a different program on TV

(3)　③　ア　speak only one language in Japan　　　　　（　　）

　　　イ　speak different languages in Japan

　　　ウ　have many people who speak Ainu in Japan

　　　エ　have very few foreigners in Japan

(4)　What is the best title of this passage?（　　　　）

　ア　Six Billion People Live on the Earth

　イ　Languages in the World

　ウ　Indian Curry

　エ　The Value of a Language

6　Read the passage and choose the answer which best completes each sentence (1)～(5).

　　There are many different kinds of caves. Some caves have been there for millions of years, but many are only a few thousands of years old. Most caves are natural — nobody made them — but some caves are artificial — they were made by people.

　　Some caves are even smaller than a small room, but some are hundreds of kilometers long. The most interesting ones have many large and small "rooms" (called chambers) with wide and narrow passages between them. They have underground rivers and waterfalls too.

　　Most natural caves were made thousands of years ago by rain water and a soft grey or white stone called limestone. Limestone is special in two ways. First, limestone contains many ① <u>cracks</u> and holes. Second, when rain water and air touch limestone, they dissolve it.

　　When rain falls on a hill, the water runs down into the small cracks and holes in the stone. It dissolves the stone and slowly makes the cracks wider. Then it runs along under the ground and carries the dissolved limestone with it. Sometimes drops of water, full of dissolved limestone, fall through the soft stone into a cave underneath. The limestone gets hard again. Slowly, many strange and beautiful shapes are made.

　　In some caves, there are natural stone bridges across underground rivers which dried up thousands of years ago. There are great waterfalls of stone. There are strange shapes like trees and flowers. The most famous shapes are stalactites and stalagmites. Stalactites come down from the roof of the cave. Stalagmites come up from the floor. When a stalagmite and a stalactite meet, they make a column. ② <u>Some chambers are so full of columns that they look like churches.</u> Most of these shapes are the same color as the limestone of the cave, but not always. If the water contains metal, the shapes can be many different colours.

（注） cave 洞くつ　　narrow passage 狭い道　　limestone 石灰岩　　contain 含む

dissolve 溶かす　　underneath 下の　　dry up 乾く　　column 柱

(1)　In this situation, the word ① cracks means （　　　）

ア　stones.

イ　rivers.

ウ　drops of water.

エ　openings.

(2)　Most caves were made （　　　）

ア　by limestone and rain water.

イ　by rain water and humans.

ウ　by metal and limestone.

エ　by humans and limestone.

(3)　To make beautiful shapes in caves, （　　　）

ア　it is necessary for rivers to run down to the limestone.

イ　it is necessary for humans to touch the cave and make cracks on limestone.

ウ　it is necessary for rain water to carry the limestone out of the cave.

エ　it is necessary for rain water and air to touch and dissolve limestone in a cave.

(4)　When we look up in the cave, （　　　）

ア　we can see stalagmites.

イ　we can see rooms and passages.

ウ　we can see stalactites.

エ　we can see trees and flowers.

(5)　In this situation, the sentence ② Some chambers are so full of columns that they look like churches. means that （　　　）

ア　some chambers are full of columns and others look like churches.

イ　some chambers look like churches because they have many columns.

ウ　some chambers are full of columns that are seen in churches.

エ　some chambers and churches have so many columns.

7   Read the passage and choose the answer which best completes each sentence (1)〜(4).

Popular breakfast foods in the United States, as in many other countries around the world, include coffee, milk, juice, eggs, and bread. Some other breakfast items served in the United States are thought by many to be traditionally American. However, they actually come from other cultures.   A

A very popular breakfast food in America is the pancake — a thin, flat cake made out of flour and often served with maple syrup.   B   In fact, pancakes were made long ago in ancient China.

Bagels, a round thick bread with a hole in the middle, are also popular for breakfast in America.   C   Polish people in the late 1600s came up with the idea for the first bagels and this new kind of bread soon took off across Eastern Europe.

In the late 1800s, thousands of Jewish people from Eastern Europe traveled to the United States and brought the recipe for bagels with ①them.   D   Today, New York bagels are said to be the best in the world. Many people have them with cream cheese for breakfast on the go.

Doughnuts (usually spelled "donut" in the United States) came from France. They were served to American soldiers in France during World War Ⅰ. After the war, American soldiers asked cooks in the United States to make doughnuts for ②them. Now, served with coffee, they are a very popular breakfast food across the United States.

(注)   include 含む   item 品目   thin 薄い   flat 平らな   flour 小麦粉
maple syrup メープルシロップ   thick 分厚い   Polish ポーランド人の
take off 急に広がる   Jewish ユダヤ人の   recipe 調理法   soldier 兵士

(1)   The word ①them refers to (   )

ア   New York bagels brought from Eastern Europe.

イ   bagels with cream cheese.

ウ   thousands of Jewish people living in New York.

エ   thousands of Jewish people from Eastern Europe.

(2)   The word ②them refers to (   )

ア   American soldiers.   イ   cooks in the United States.

ウ   popular breakfast foods.   エ   doughnuts served in France.

(3)   The sentence "The idea of the pancake is very old." should be put in (   )

ア   A .   イ   B .   ウ   C .   エ   D .

(4) The best title for this passage is （　　　）

　ア　Famous places to eat breakfast.

　イ　The history of popular breakfast foods in the United States.

　ウ　The most popular types of pancakes in the United States.

　エ　Why people in the United States eat breakfast.

8 Read the passage and choose the answer which best completes each sentence (1)〜(4).

　　Today, most people in their twenties have smartphones. They use smartphones not only as a communication tool, but also as a personal computer. A smartphone has a lot of useful things, for example, a clock, a calendar, the Internet, a calculator, maps, a camera, a music player, and so on. ☐A☐ If people forget their phones at home in the morning, they will often run back for ①them. They don't mind being late for their jobs or classes. It's difficult to imagine life without this small machine.

　　There are many advantages to using a smartphone. It is now simple to use the Internet, so young people can do research for their homework quickly and easily. ☐B☐ This often helps teenagers get more information without going to the library or looking words up in a paper dictionary.

　　People can find places they haven't been to before more easily if they use navigation applications. Also, thanks to SNS, we can communicate with friends and family around the world anytime and anywhere. In fact, new smartphone applications are being made every day, so this small device can become even more useful.

　　On the other hand, there are some negative points. Some children play online games and waste too many hours each day. They should do more outdoor activities and do their homework. In some families, people even use their smartphones at the dinner table, so they do not talk to each other. Do you know what is happening? ☐C☐

　　People have a lot of personal information on their smartphones. If the device is lost, ②it could be a serious problem. All of that personal information may be in danger of being stolen by someone else. Isn't that scary?

　　We are now living in a world of technology. Smartphones are very useful in our daily lives and they are so convenient that we cannot live without them. ☐D☐ However, we should be careful and use these devices wisely.

(注)　calculator　計算機　　imagine　想像する　　advantages　利点

application　携帯用のソフトウエアー

SNS　LINE や Facebook などのソーシャルネットワーキングサービス　　device　装置

negative　否定的な　　scary　おそろしい　　convenient　便利な

(1)　The word ① them refers to （　　　）

ア　their phones.

イ　their jobs.

ウ　their classes.

エ　their personal computers.

(2)　The word ② it means （　　　）

ア　people's personal information on their smartphones.

イ　that people's personal information is dangerous.

ウ　that the smartphone is lost.

エ　that someone may steal people's personal information.

(3)　The sentence "Smartphones are used for communication but they are actually becoming walls that stop people from communicating face to face." should be put in （　　　）

ア　A .　　イ　B .　　ウ　C .　　エ　D .

(4)　The best title for this passage is （　　　）

ア　The usefulness of smartphones.

イ　How each age group uses smartphones.

ウ　How bad it is to use smartphones on a train.

エ　Good and bad points of using smartphones.

§3. 短い英文を読む問題②

1 Read the passage and choose the answer which best completes each sentence (1)〜(4).

Cultural heritage is not limited to things that we can actually see or touch. It also includes culturally important local knowledge, skills, and customs. To protect and respect such intangible cultural heritage, UNESCO makes a list of them. In 2019, 42 things in 55 countries were added to the list.

Traditional Thai massage was one of ① them. It is known as part of the art, science, and culture of traditional knowledge for health in the country. The therapists give you a good stretch and you can really relax after that. It is popular all over the world and you can also find therapists here in Japan.

Another example is a local festival in the village of Podence in Portugal. It was also added to the list in 2019. The traditional festival is held every winter and it ② for over three days. Men, women, and children enjoy it at the end of winter and the beginning of spring.

People who wear masks or colorful costumes with bells walk through the village during the festival. They sometimes dance or go around the homes of their friends or neighbors. But many people who know the festival probably agree that one of the most exciting moments is burning a doll which looks like a devil. It is the cleaning process of bad things through fire.

> (注) cultural heritage 文化遺産　 limit 限定する　 include 含む　 culturally 文化的に
> knowledge 知識　 skill 技術　 intangible 無形の　 UNESCO ユネスコ
> Thai massage タイマッサージ　 therapist セラピスト　 stretch ストレッチ
> Podence ポデンセ　 Portugal ポルトガル　 beginning 始まり　 mask マスク
> colorful カラフルな　 bell 鈴　 probably たぶん　 devil 悪魔
> cleaning process 浄化プロセス

(1) According to the passage, UNESCO makes a list of intangible cultural heritage because
(　　)
ア　they thought that respecting Western culture is important.
イ　they wanted to see or touch them.
ウ　they respect people who know world culture well enough.
エ　they want to protect various important cultures all over the world.

(2)　The word ① them refers to （　　　）

ア　lists that include culturally important people in 2019.

イ　skills and customs that were first found in 2019.

ウ　things that were added to the list in 2019.

エ　countries that made the list in 2019.

(3)　The word which should be put in ② is （　　　）

ア　ends.　　イ　continues.　　ウ　responds.　　エ　looks.

(4)　According to the passage, during the festival of Podence, （　　　）

ア　people dance a lot after burning a doll.

イ　people in colorful clothes walk through the village.

ウ　people throw necessary things into fire.

エ　people greet each other to find devils inside them.

2　Read the passage and choose the answer which best completes each sentence (1)〜(4).

　　We all know that any person has a dream while they are sleeping.　We also know that it is difficult to remember dreams after we wake up.　Most dreams are soon forgotten and they disappear like small bubbles in water.　In addition, ① they often cannot be remembered at all after they are forgotten.　Even if you can remember a dream soon after you wake up, perhaps you cannot remember it any more after getting out from your bed to make some coffee.　Maybe you have had such an experience.

　　Then, have you ever noticed that you were having a dream while you were sleeping?　Some people have had such an experience.　It is called a lucid dream, and some scientists in the world do research on it.　Actually, there are even research groups which focus on it.

　　Why do they do research on lucid dreams?　For one thing, there may be advantages for us.　We will be able to avoid nightmares and make our dreams happier or more exciting if we can notice we are having dreams and we can control them like a pilot.　Today, scientists do not know enough about lucid dreams and how to control them, so there are still many things to be done in the research.　But it may be possible for everyone to have lucid dreams if science in the area improves more.　Actually, that is one of goals that some scientists are trying to reach.

According to a survey, over 75% of the respondents answered that they experienced a lucid dream at least once in their lives. Also, many reports about lucid dream experiences were given in history. We can find early reports on them in books from ancient cultures. For example, an ancient Greek doctor already tried to use lucid dreams as a kind of therapy over two thousand years ago. And controlling our dreams in our own ways was one of the important topics among early Buddhists in Asia.

（注）　while ～　～する間に　　bubble　泡　　even if ～　たとえ～でも　　perhaps　たぶん
lucid dream　明晰夢　　focus on ～　～に特化する　　for one thing　一つには
avoid　避ける　　nightmare　悪夢　　control　制御する　　pilot　パイロット
survey　調査　　respondent　回答者　　at least　少なくとも　　early　初期の
ancient　古代の　　Greek　ギリシャ　　therapy　治療　　topic　テーマ
Buddhist　仏教徒

(1) The word ① they refers to （　　　）

ア　most dreams that we have while we are sleeping.
イ　most people who have several dreams in one night.
ウ　a few things that we can do when we feel sleepy.
エ　people who can remember their dreams well.

(2) According to the passage, （　　　）

ア　pilots often fly in their dreams while they are sleeping.
イ　studying lucid dreams has good and bad sides.
ウ　lucid dreams have been a research topic for some people.
エ　drinking some coffee is helpful for remembering dreams.

(3) In the future, （　　　）

ア　lucid dreams may be forgotten from everyone's memory.
イ　some research groups will focus on the bad side of lucid dreams.
ウ　25% of people will be able to have lucid dreams.
エ　we may stop having bad dreams and be able to control them.

(4) According to the passage, there are a lot of reports on lucid dream experiences, （　　　）

ア　but many people in Asia did not know what they were for many centuries.
イ　and early ones can be found in old culture.
ウ　and an Ancient Greek doctor was able to avoid nightmares.
エ　but scientists know that most of them are not true reports.

3　Read the passage and choose the answer which best completes each sentence (1)～(4).

　　Among various animal species, electric eels are perhaps known as one of the most amazing and dangerous ones.　They live in the rivers of South America.　Maybe you have seen them on TV, videos on the Internet, or in aquariums.　If you have ever seen them, you know that they are quite different from eels although they have the word "eel" in their name.　Actually, they are classified into a group that is called "knifefish" and cannot be eaten like eels.

　　Electric eels can grow up to 250 cm in length.　When you think about the fact that the common length of Japanese eels is about 40 cm, you know that electric eels are quite long animals.　But the most amazing feature of electric eels is the fact that they can shock other animals by 　①　 about 600 volts of electricity.　It is strong enough to kill them.　For your information, most outlets in Japan are for 100 volts.　Dry cells that you use for your TV remote controller generate 1.5 volts of electricity.　You can imagine how strong their attack is.

　　Although the attack continues only for a moment, it is very strong.　But, 　　②　　 in the first place? It is said that it is generated from thousands of muscle cells all over their bodies.　Each muscle cell generates only about 0.15 volts of electricity.　If thousands of them work together, however, it can even reach 900 volts of electricity.

　　It is also said that electric eels can use another type of electricity.　It is weaker, but they need it for their dinner.　Because they cannot see things very well, they first look for food like small fish by using their weak type of electricity.　After they find their target, their attack begins.　They "cook" their food by using their strong type of electricity and they enjoy eating it.

　　(注)　species　種　　electric eel　電気ウナギ　　perhaps　たぶん　　aquarium　水族館
　　　　　eel　ウナギ　　classify　分類する　　knifefish　ナイフフィッシュ　　length　長さ
　　　　　the fact that ～　～という事実　　common　普通の　　feature　特徴
　　　　　shock　電気ショックを与える　　volt　ボルト　　outlet　コンセント　　dry cell　乾電池
　　　　　remote controller　リモコン　　generate　生み出す　　attack　攻撃
　　　　　in the first place　そもそも　　thousands of ～　何千もの～　　muscle cell　筋肉細胞
　　　　　target　ターゲット

(1)　Electric eels are amazing and dangerous species and they （　　　　）
　　ア　are in a different group from eels and cannot be cooked.
　　イ　could not be found in aquariums until recently.
　　ウ　can live without water for several hours.
　　エ　are hard to catch but their taste is very good.

(2)　The word which should be put in ┌ ① ┐ is （　　　）

ア　eating.　　イ　producing.　　ウ　accepting.　　エ　refusing.

(3)　What is the sentence which should be put in ┌ ② ┐? （　　　）

　　ア　how many electric eels are there in the world

　　イ　how many volts of electricity are dangerous to animals

　　ウ　where does this electricity come from

　　エ　where are electric eels born

(4)　According to the passage, （　　　）

　　ア　electric eels are able to see and hear things clearly even in water.

　　イ　electric eels use two types of electricity when they decide to eat something.

　　ウ　it is known that Japanese eels can also generate a weak type of electricity.

　　エ　it is said that Japanese eels are sometimes eaten by electric eels.

4　Read the passage and choose the answer which best completes each sentence (1)～(4).

　　In 1931, a large conch shell was found in a cave in France. The cave is famous for its old wall paintings. It is in the mountains, and not close to the ocean — the nearest sea from the cave is over 200 kilometers away. The conch shell was about 30 centimeters long. People who ┌ ① ┐ it thought that it was a cup for drinking. It was later given to a French museum, and people paid little attention to it until recently.

a conch shell
（ほら貝）

　　According to some French research in 2021, the conch shell was played ┌ ② ┐ a musical instrument such as a horn. The latest technology helped them realize that this conch shell was actually a musical instrument, and not a cup for drinking. To confirm this hypothesis, a horn player was invited to the research group. They asked the musician to blow the conch shell and it produced three clear sounds.

　　The research shows that the conch shell is about 18,000 years old, and there are three interesting points about it. First, one end of the conch shell had holes. Scientists who joined the research said that this was probably intentional because the holes were in the hardest part of the conch shell. Someone probably made the holes to put something like a mouthpiece in it to blow. Second, there were some cut parts at the other end. These parts can help people put their hands in the shell and change their pitch easily. Finally, there are red dot-like patterns inside the conch shell. These patterns were similar to those of paintings in the cave.

These three points showed that the conch shell was processed by humans for a reason. This was probably for improving its sound, or for playing it as a musical instrument during ceremonies. This old musical instrument tells us that humans enjoyed music a long, long time ago.

(注)　cave　洞窟　　musical instrument　楽器　　horn　ホルン（管楽器）　　realize　〜に気づく
confirm　〜を裏づける　　hypothesis　仮説　　blow　〜を鳴らす　　hole　穴
intentional　意図的な　　mouthpiece　マウスピース（管楽器の口の部分に当てる物）
cut　切断された　　pitch　（音の）高低　　dot-like　点のような　　pattern　模様
process　〜を加工する　　ceremony　儀式

(1)　The word which should be put in 　①　 is （　　　）

　ア　wasted.　　イ　supported.　　ウ　discovered.　　エ　protected.

(2)　The word which should be put in 　②　 is （　　　）

　ア　with.　　イ　as.　　ウ　behind.　　エ　through.

(3)　The research group wanted to confirm their hypothesis, so （　　　）

　ア　a French scientist took horn lessons from a famous musician.

　イ　they asked a musician to play the large conch shell.

　ウ　they looked for volunteers to help in their research.

　エ　they bought a horn to compare the musical instruments.

(4)　According to the passage, （　　　）

　ア　changes made in both ends of the conch shell probably had a purpose.

　イ　the red dot-like patterns and holes inside the conch shell were added after it was given to a French museum in the twentieth century.

　ウ　people who lived in the cave in France about 18,000 years ago used conch shells to cut hard things that they wanted to eat.

　エ　at first, the conch shell was probably used by people for drinking something in old times, but the way to use it was changed later.

5 Read the passage and choose the answer which best completes each sentence (1)～(3) and choose the answer to the question (4).

chopsticks
（箸）

Chopsticks are used in China, Korea, and Japan. The chopsticks used in these three countries are different and each has unique features.

Chinese chopsticks are long and thick, and their ends are not pointed. Chinese people traditionally sit around a large round table together and ⬚① food. They usually pick up food from the same dish, so it is helpful for them to use long and thick chopsticks.

The chopsticks that Korean people usually use are heavy and strong. The reason can be found in the materials. In old times, chopsticks made of silver were used by kings in Korea and China. People believed that they could find poison in food by using silver chopsticks and watching the change in color. ⬚A Today, most chopsticks used in Korea are made of stainless steel. ⬚B Steel chopsticks are popular because their surfaces are shiny, and they are like mirrors. ⬚C In Korea, chopsticks are usually set with a spoon on the table because Korean people eat rice with spoons. ⬚D

How about Japanese chopsticks? ⬚② They are usually lacquered, so they last long and many people appreciate its beauty. So, they are often chosen as gifts especially for people living outside Japan.

（注）　unique　独特の　　feature　特徴　　thick　太い　　pointed　先の尖った

traditionally　伝統的に　　material　材料　　poison　毒　　stainless steel　ステンレス鋼

surface　表面　　shiny　ぴかぴかの　　mirror　鏡　　lacquer　～に漆を塗る

appreciate　～の真価を認める　　beauty　美

(1) The word which should be put in ⬚① is （　　　）

ア　add.　　イ　carry.　　ウ　share.　　エ　set.

(2) In Korea, chopsticks made of silver were used in old times because （　　　）

ア　their shiny surface could be used as mirrors.

イ　silver was more expensive than any other material.

ウ　kings in Korea and China liked its color.

エ　people thought they could use it to find poison in food.

(3) The sentence "In addition, it is easy to wash them again and again." should be put in

（　　　）

ア　⬚A .　　イ　⬚B .　　ウ　⬚C .　　エ　⬚D .

(4)　The following passages （ⅰ）〜（ⅳ） should be put in 　②　 in the order that makes the most sense. （　　）

（ⅰ）　Why do Japanese chopsticks have pointed ends, then?　They have pointed ends because they are convenient for eating fish.　These chopsticks can help us remove the bones.

（ⅱ）　We can find the reasons for this in Japanese food customs.　Japanese chopsticks are short because Japanese people traditionally do not share food in the same dish.

（ⅲ）　Because of their shape, we can eat fish in a safe way.　Another interesting feature of Japanese chopsticks is their surface.

（ⅳ）　Japanese chopsticks are short and light.　Also, they have pointed ends.

　　（注）　bone　骨

Which is the best order?

　　ア　（ⅳ）→（ⅰ）→（ⅱ）→（ⅲ）　　　イ　（ⅳ）→（ⅱ）→（ⅰ）→（ⅲ）
　　ウ　（ⅰ）→（ⅱ）→（ⅳ）→（ⅲ）　　　エ　（ⅰ）→（ⅳ）→（ⅱ）→（ⅲ）

6　Read the passage and choose the answer which best completes each sentence (1)〜(4).

　　The number of farmers is decreasing in Japan.　One of the reasons is that the things farmers have to do every day are hard and sometimes dangerous.　Some of the work such as driving a tractor needs special skills and experience.　However, this situation can be improved by "smart farming."　This means using the latest technology such as machines, AIs, and systems in farming.　By using it, ①they can make some of their work automatic, and get and share information about crops more easily.

　　One example is an automatic tractor.　This tractor does not need a driver.　It has a sensor which can find things in front of the car, so it is 　②　 to use.　Another example is a machine which can mow grass.　It is also automatic, small, and does not need a driver.　According to an estimate, by using the machine, people who need 225 hours to mow grass can do the same work in 75 hours.　In addition, there are machines which can 　③　 fruits and vegetables without drivers.

　　In Japan, to see how helpful smart farming is, a project was started in 2019.　In this project, the latest technology is used in 179 farming areas in Japan (as of April, 2021).　The way to use smart farming is different from area to area.　For example, in the Kinki region, smart farming is used in seven areas for fruit production, while it is only used in one area for the same purpose in the Hokuriku region.　In the Hokuriku region, smart farming is used for dry field farming and growing animals, and it is used in about 10 farming areas for paddy farming. It is also used for gardening and growing flowers.

It is true that there are some difficulties in smart farming, such as costs and infrastructure. However, it will grow in the near future, and change the way of farming.

（注）　decrease　減る　　tractor　トラクター　　smart farming　スマート農業　　AI　人工知能
farming　農業　　automatic　自動の　　crop　作物　　sensor　センサー　　mow　～を刈る
grass　草　　estimate　推定　　project　計画　　as of ～　～時点で
Kinki region　近畿地方　　production　生産　　while　～であるのに対し…
Hokuriku region　北陸地方　　dry field farming　畑作　　paddy farming　水田作
gardening　園芸　　cost　コスト　　infrastructure　インフラ

(1) The word ① they refers to （　　　）
　ア　machines.　　イ　jobs.　　ウ　farmers.　　エ　fruits and vegetables.

(2) The word which should be put in ② is （　　　）
　ア　safe.　　イ　traditional.　　ウ　noisy.　　エ　impossible.

(3) The word which should be put in ③ is （　　　）
　ア　compare.　　イ　greet.　　ウ　order.　　エ　collect.

(4) According to an estimate in the passage, （　　　）
　ア　it took over 75 hours for people to invent a machine which is now used to mow grass.
　イ　people who work in farming can finish mowing grass more quickly by using machines.
　ウ　over 150 machines which are helpful for farmers will be developed in the near future.
　エ　over 200 farming areas in Japan use the latest technology as of April, 2021.

§4. 長い英文を読む問題

1 Read the passage and choose the answer which best completes each sentence (1)〜(5).

The newspaper said that four endangered birds were killed in a wild bird area by hunters who thought they were killing *Pukekos. Pukekos* live in every place in New Zealand. It is very easy to see them on roadsides and in fields all around New Zealand.

The rangers, who work to take care of a park, said that some hunters shot four *Takahes*, which are endangered birds in New Zealand. The hunters were killing 600 *Pukekos* which lived in a bird area for endangered birds.

That big mistake makes people in New Zealand angry because they agreed to carry the endangered birds to safe places.

The *Takahes* were killed by members of the local deer-hunters group. One of the members said *Pukekos* were a very similar color to *Takahes* and the volunteers didn't understand the two birds. Both are about 50 cm long.

However, the hunters were told about the differences between the two birds after a similar accident on the island some years ago, when one *Takahe* was killed. The death was very sad for volunteers and rangers. So they had long meetings. Now there are only 300 *Takahes* in New Zealand and *Takahes* are known as an "endangered bird."

Takahes are birds which cannot fly. Their wings are too short to fly. Why can *Takahes* live in New Zealand? Many years ago, there were no big animals which can eat them for food and it was safe to stay on the ground. Their favorite food is plant leaves, weeds, and seeds. They sometimes eat insects. They became birds which don't have to fly. However, humans came from other countries to cross the sea, and big problems happened. The animals which people took there killed and ate them and stole their food. The numbers of *Takahes* are getting smaller. In order to save *Takahes* from extinction people in New Zealand are trying to protect them. They have removed *Ermines* which usually kill *Takahes* for food and deer which usually eat a lot of plant leaves. They protect and raise the eggs which *Takahes* lay. They leave adult *Takahes* in the field when they grow up. They protect the environment for *Takahes*.

Pukekos are one of the most common birds in New Zealand. They can be seen on every roadside in the country. They look like *Takahes*, so it is difficult to know which are *Pukekos* or *Takahes*. Both birds are about 50 cm long and they are vegetarians. Their faces are very similar. But one of the differences is color; *Pukekos* have a deep blue color, on the other hand *Takahes* have a lighter blue color than *Pukekos*. Another difference is that *Pukekos* can fly. This is a big difference. *Pukekos* can escape from the enemy into the sky, but 　①　 cannot.

Pukekos give New Zealand a headache. The numbers of them are getting bigger, so

Pukekos live in more fields which other birds want to live in. The smaller birds cannot live near ② because there is not enough space.

  Both *Takahes* and *Pukekos* are native birds in New Zealand. People want to protect them. How can we help *Takahes* and *Pukekos*?

（注） endangered 絶滅の危機にさらされている hunter ハンター，狩りをする人

    pukeko プケコ（鳥の名前） New Zealand ニュージーランド roadside 道ばた

    ranger レンジャー shot shoot（銃で撃つ）の過去形 *takahe* タカへ（鳥の名前）

    deer 鹿 wing 翼 weed 雑草 seed 種 insect 昆虫 cross 渡る

    stole steal（奪う）の過去形 extinction 絶滅 *ermine* オコジョ（イタチの一種）

    raise 育てる common よく見られる vegetarian 菜食者 escape 逃げる

    enemy 敵 native 原産の

(1) The expression which should be put in ① is（   ）

 ア hunters. イ *Pukekos*. ウ *Takahes*. エ *Takahes* and *Pukekos*.

(2) The expression which should be put in ② is（   ）

 ア hunters. イ *Pukekos*. ウ *Takahes*. エ *Takahes* and *Pukekos*.

(3) Some hunters shot four *Takahes* because（   ）

 ア they thought *Takahes* were not endangered birds.

 イ they did not think they were *Takahes*.

 ウ they could be seen on roadsides around New Zealand.

 エ they are about 50 cm long.

(4) *Takahes'* wings are too short because（   ）

 ア their favorite food is insects and seeds.

 イ people in New Zealand are protecting them.

 ウ it was not dangerous to live on the ground in New Zealand.

 エ humans from other countries did not kill them.

(5) According to the passage,（   ）

 ア we can easily see *Pukekos* on roadsides in New Zealand.

 イ the rangers in New Zealand killed *Takahes* in a bird area.

 ウ both *Takahes* and *Pukekos* can eat smaller animals.

 エ *Takahes* are born in New Zealand but *Pukekos* are not.

2 Read the passage and choose the answer which best completes each sentence (1)〜(5).

When you think of a robot, what do you see? A machine that looks a bit like you and me? Actually, robots have in many different shapes and sizes. They don't have to look like humans — in fact, ⬚①⬚ .

Robots look different from each other because they are made for different purposes. Flying robots may look like helicopters, or have wings like insects or birds. Cleaning robots often look like little vacuums. Robots that are made to communicate with people often have a face, eyes, or a mouth — just like we do!

Most robots have three important parts: sensors, actuators and programs. Together, these three parts make a robot different from other electronic equipment you have around your house, like your computer, your washing machine, or your TV.

First, a robot has sensors to help it notice the world around it. Just like we have eyes to notice light, ears to notice sound, and nerves in our skin to notice something that is touching us, robots have light sensors and cameras so they can " ⬚②⬚ ," microphones so they can "hear," and pressure sensors so they can "feel" the things around them.

Second, a robot has actuators to move around. We use our legs and feet to walk and run, and we use our hands to pick up a ball and throw it. A robot uses actuators such as motors and wheels or the parts which look like fingers, so they can drive and move around, or hold objects and control them or turn them around.

Third, a robot needs a program to follow in order to act or do the next thing when it notices something. This ability to act by itself is called autonomy. Let's look at this idea of autonomy.

Can you think of anything that has autonomy? People have autonomy because they can decide for themselves how to behave or move most of the time. Your TV, or your washing machine is an example of the machines that ⬚③⬚ , because they depend on a person to make decisions for them.

When a robot has autonomy, it is a little different from the autonomy a person has, because a person has to write the computer program that tells the robot what to do. For example, when we listen to music, our brains tell us how to move our own legs to the music — we don't need someone to move our legs for us!

But if we want to build a robot that can dance to music all by itself, what three things do we need? We need sensors, actuators and program to dance.

We also need a computer — the robot's brain — that can notice all the information and run the program, and some kind of batteries to give electricity to our robot.

Some robots can do many different things. Cars that have autonomy, for example, have good sensors so they can find how far it is to all the things around them and build a

3-dimensional (3-D) map of the area. Then they also have a good program that understands the situation in the map: How many cars are there? Where are the roads and other things in the 3D map? When it carefully understands the situation, the program controls the robot's speed and movement.

（注）　robot　ロボット　　a bit　少し　　helicopter　ヘリコプター　　wing　羽　　insect　昆虫

vacuum　掃除機　　sensor　センサー　　actuator　作動装置　　program　プログラム

electronic equipment　電化製品　　washing machine　洗濯機　　nerve　神経　　skin　肌

microphone　マイク　　pressure　圧力　　motor　モーター　　wheel　車輪　　ability　能力

autonomy　オートノミー，自律性　　behave　振る舞う　　make decisions　決定をする

brain　脳　　run　（コンピュータープログラムを）動かす　　battery　バッテリー

3-dimensional　三次元の　　speed　速さ　　movement　動き

(1)　The phrase which should be put in ①　is（　　　）

　ア　most robots look like humans.　　イ　most robots don't look like humans.

　ウ　most humans look like robots.　　エ　most humans don't look like robots.

(2)　The word which should be put in ②　is（　　　）

　ア　see.　　イ　listen.　　ウ　touch.　　エ　calculate.

(3)　The phrase which should be put in ③　is（　　　）

　ア　have autonomy.　　イ　don't have autonomy.　　ウ　can decide how to behave.

　エ　can decide how to move.

(4)　According to the passage, cars that have autonomy can（　　　）

　ア　write the computer program.

　イ　build a robot that can dance to music.

　ウ　make some kind of batteries to give electricity.

　エ　carefully study the situation in the map.

(5)　According to the passage,（　　　）

　ア　robots which can communicate with people don't have a face, eyes, or a mouth.

　イ　electronic equipments which people have around their houses have sensors, actuators and programs.

　ウ　the autonomy people have is a little different from the one robots have.

　エ　a computer is not necessary to make a robot which can dance to music all by itself.

3 Read the passage and choose the answer which best completes each sentence (1), (3), (4) and (5), and choose the answer to the question (2).

　　An English dictionary is one of the most important things you will use when you learn English. A good dictionary will help you learn hundreds of new words and how to use them. When you think of a dictionary, you usually think of a bilingual dictionary. A bilingual dictionary is a two-language dictionary, like an English-Japanese dictionary or a Japanese-English dictionary. In English-Japanese dictionaries, English words are explained in Japanese, and in Japanese-English dictionaries, Japanese words are explained in English. These are very powerful tools for us, but there is also another kind of dictionary: a monolingual dictionary. A monolingual dictionary is a one-language dictionary, like an English-English dictionary. This type of dictionary is written only in English, so English words are not translated; they are explained in 　①　 . They may look difficult at first, but I'll tell you many good points about English-English dictionaries.

　　First, if you use monolingual dictionaries, you will be more careful about how to use new words. 　　②　　 Since every explanation is in English, it gives you a clearer understanding of how to use the new words. Moreover, since monolingual dictionaries show you how to use a word in sentences, they show you which words are often used with the new words that you are looking up.

　　Second, if you use monolingual dictionaries, you will look up words more often than if you use bilingual dictionaries. You may not know all the words in the definitions, and then you use the dictionary again. For example, if you look up the word "excavate", you'll see the definition saying "dig carefully to find ancient things." If you don't know the words "dig" or "ancient," you will have to look ③ them up. "Dig" is explained as "make a hole in the ground." "Ancient" means "coming from very long ago." So instead of one word, you can learn three words! In this way, when you find words you don't know in the definition, you need to look up these new words to understand the meaning. This gives you a lot of chances to improve your English.

　　Lastly, English-English dictionaries explain words in simple English, so you don't have to be afraid of using them. When people make an English-English dictionary, they usually choose 2000 to 3000 words which they use for definitions (usually the chosen words are very 　④　 and very useful words), and they use only those words in their dictionary. Also, you can find the list of the words they have chosen at the last section of the dictionary. So if you study the list and use the dictionary over and over, you will learn the most important English words before you know it!

　　So maybe now you clearly see how useful English-English dictionaries can be. It may look too difficult at first, but if you want to be really good at English, monolingual dictionaries will be very helpful.

> （注）　bilingual　二言語を用いる　　powerful　力強い　　tool　ツール
>
> monolingual　一言語だけを用いる　　translate　翻訳する，別の言語で言い換える
>
> explanation　説明　　look up　（辞書で）調べる　　definition　定義，説明
>
> excavate　発掘する　　dig　掘る　　ancient　古代の　　hole　穴
>
> instead of ～　～の代わりに，～ではなく　　lastly　最後に　　section　部分
>
> over and over　何度も

(1)　The expression which should be put in ｜　①　｜ is （　　　）

　　ア　English and Japanese.　　イ　English.　　ウ　Japanese.　　エ　Japanese and French.

(2)　The following passage （ⅰ）～（ⅲ）should be put in ｜　②　｜ in the order that makes the most sense. （　　　）

　（ⅰ）　If you use monolingual dictionaries, you will have to read explanations and example sentences written in English over and over.

　（ⅱ）　When we use English-Japanese dictionaries, many of us just look at explanations in Japanese.

　（ⅲ）　It is fast, but in many cases, only looking at Japanese explanations doesn't help us learn English.

　　　　ア　（ⅰ）→（ⅱ）→（ⅲ）　　イ　（ⅰ）→（ⅲ）→（ⅱ）

　　　　ウ　（ⅱ）→（ⅰ）→（ⅲ）　　エ　（ⅱ）→（ⅲ）→（ⅰ）

(3)　The words ③them refers to （　　　）

　　ア　the definitions.　　イ　ancient things.　　ウ　the words "dig" or "ancient."

　　エ　three words.

(4)　The word which should be put in ｜　④　｜ is （　　　）

　　ア　difficult.　　イ　unknown.　　ウ　simple.　　エ　interesting.

(5)　According to the passage, （　　　）

　　ア　many people think of a bilingual dictionary when they think of a dictionary.

　　イ　a Japanese-English dictionary is one example of a monolingual dictionary.

　　ウ　a bilingual dictionary will give you more chances to improve your English than a monolingual dictionary.

　　エ　you will not find any list of the words in a monolingual dictionary.

4　Read the passage and choose the answer which best completes each sentence (1)〜(5).

　　Long, long ago, dinosaurs lived on Earth. They walked with heavy steps on the ground, swam in the water and flew over the fields. This was millions of years ago and this time lasted for about 165 million years. But one day, they disappeared and never came back. Dinosaurs died out, but some other species survived. It was difficult for them to adapt to the changes in the environment. We are here now because of this.

　　For many different reasons, it is difficult for some species to live in their environment and they can no longer continue the next generation; each of these species will die out and after a few years, we will not be able to find any of them on Earth. This is the 'extinction' of that species. When animals or plants are in danger of extinction, they are called 'endangered species'.

　　There are many reasons for extinction. Before human beings appeared, extinction happened often. When one species could not survive in a changing environment, it became extinct. Scientists say that about 99.9% of all species that have lived on Earth are now extinct. Since human beings appeared, especially since history was written and kept, most extinction has occurred because of human activities.

The main causes of extinction by humans are:
- Hunting too much: one species is hunted for food, science and other such things because they are necessary.
- Killing for safety and business: all of a species is killed to protect pets, farm animals and crops.
- Taking species as pets: a species is caught by humans to use as pets and taken from their natural world.
- Pollution: because of industrial waste, the home of a species becomes no longer safe and the species becomes extinct.
- Deforestation: forests and fields are cleared and are used to make money from selling houses and so species lose their home and become extinct.

　　Because of these causes, many species are in danger. Before the Industrial Revolution, the main cause of extinction of a species was killing too much through hunting. But, after the Industrial Revolution, destroying species' homes has become the main cause. Losing not only a large area, but even small changes to a species' home can cause its extinction. This is because it stops the species from moving around and communicating with each other. This becomes a big problem for the species because it is not able to reproduce. For example, scientists say that building just a few roads can stop China's pandas from meeting each other. Pandas do not cross roads. When some bridges were built for the pandas to move, their numbers increased a little again.

As our world has become smaller through communication between countries, it has also caused extinction. Development of travel between countries has meant that many animals travel around the world with humans and therefore hurt native species of many countries. People around the world enjoy having animals and plants that are from far away places. It means that many animals are at risk. Every year, a lot of animals and plants are brought from developing countries to rich, developed countries. Because of this give and take between countries, a lot of animals are caught and sent to foreign countries just for people's enjoyment.

Polar bears, pandas, gorillas, tigers, and many kinds of plants are all well-known to us today, but if we do not do something soon, the only way for our children to see them will be in books and old TV shows.

（注）　dinosaur　恐竜　　die out　絶滅する　　species　種　　adapt to　に適応する
no longer　もはや〜ない　　generation　世代　　extinction　絶滅
endangered species　絶滅危惧種　　extinct　絶滅した　　occur　起こる　　cause　原因
hunt　狩る，狩猟する　　safety　安全　　crop　作物　　pollution　汚染
industrial waste　産業廃棄物　　deforestation　森林破壊　　clear　取り除く
the Industrial Revolution　産業革命　　reproduce　繁殖する　　cross　横断する
development　発達　　therefore　その結果　　native　固有の　　at risk　危険にひんしている
give and take　やりとり　　enjoyment　楽しみ　　polar bears　北極グマ　　panda　パンダ
gorilla　ゴリラ　　well-known　よく知られている

(1)　Dinosaurs　（　　　　）
　　ア　are an example of a species that has become extinct.
　　イ　were killed by human beings a hundred years ago.
　　ウ　ate all the other species on Earth about 165 million years ago.
　　エ　are an endangered species.

(2)　Almost 100%　（　　　　）
　　ア　of all dinosaurs that have lived on Earth can fly over the fields.
　　イ　of animals that have lived as pets are wonderful because they are expensive.
　　ウ　of animals and plants that have lived on Earth are not seen now.
　　エ　of animals and plants that have lived have caused all extinctions on Earth.

(3)　One of the reasons for extinction is that（　　　）

　　ア　humans hunt many kinds of dinosaurs for food.

　　イ　humans cut trees and build houses to make more money.

　　ウ　volunteers save forests and fields.

　　エ　people always like to travel abroad with their pets.

(4)　Polar bears, pandas, gorillas, tigers, and many kinds of plants（　　　）

　　ア　became extinct hundreds of years ago.

　　イ　are endangered species because there are so many of them.

　　ウ　are the most important species that we should save.

　　エ　may disappear if human beings do not try to protect the environment.

(5)　According to the passage,（　　　）

　　ア　many native animals hurt other species in their native country.

　　イ　almost all kinds of animals and plants cannot survive over millions of years.

　　ウ　since humans appeared in history, the number of species that have become extinct has become smaller.

　　エ　some species will become extinct because of books and TV shows.

5　Read the passage and choose the answer to the question (1), and choose the answer which best completes each sentence (2)～(5).

　　Paul was born in a rich family. His family lived in New York and his father ran five restaurants. When Paul was two years old, his mother died. So he had no memory of his mother. His father never had a wife again.

　　Paul had a brother, Tom. He was ten years older than Paul. When Paul was five years old, their father opened five more restaurants. He became very busy. He wanted to come home every day and spend much time with them, but he couldn't. So Tom took care of Paul very well.

　　Tom began to help his father with his business when Paul was twelve years old. _____①_____ . And on Christmas Eve, he bought anything Paul wanted. But Paul didn't buy any gifts for Tom because he didn't have enough money. When Paul said with a smile, "Thank you. I like it very much. I'm sorry I can't give you any gifts," Tom always said, "That's OK. Your smile makes me happier than to receive any gifts."

When Paul was eighteen years old, he received a car from Tom ② a Christmas gift. A few days later, just before Christmas Eve, he got a driver's license. When Paul went out of his house to go for a drive on Christmas Eve, a boy was walking around the new car and asked, "Is this your car?"

"Yes. My brother gave it to me for Christmas," Paul answered. The boy was surprised and said, "You mean your brother gave it to you and you paid nothing? Oh, I want to...."

Of course Paul knew the words the boy was trying to say. Paul thought he was going to say, "Oh, I want to have a brother like him." But Paul was surprised at the words the boy said. He said, "I want to be like your brother."

Paul did not know him, but he thought he was a good boy. Paul liked him, so he asked, "Would you like to ride in my car?" "Yes, yes!" the boy answered. They got into the car and went for a drive.

After a while, the boy said, "Would you take me to my house in this car?" Paul smiled and said, "Of course." Paul thought the boy wanted to show his neighbors that he could ride home in a big car. But Paul was ③ again. "Will you stop the car in front of the house which has two steps?" the boy asked.

After he got out of the car, he ran up the steps and went into the house. Then in a little while he came back slowly. He was carrying his younger brother. He could not walk by himself. They sat on the bottom step together. The boy pointed to the car.

"That is the car I told you about in the house. His brother gave it to him for Christmas and he paid nothing. Someday I'm going to give you a car like that. Then you can see for yourself all the pretty things for Christmas that I told you about again and again." Paul almost cried when he heard this.

Paul got out of the car and carried the boy's brother into the front seat of his car. The boy sat next to his brother and three of them went for a drive. Paul took them to the center of the city and showed them the beautiful windows of the shops. The boy's brother rode in a car and went there for the first time in his life. Everything he saw was new to him. He was very excited. The boy smiled at him. It made Paul very happy. It was a wonderful time.

"It is more blessed to ④ ," Tom always said to Paul. That Christmas Eve, Paul understood that reason.

（注） ran run（経営する）の過去形　cared care（気にかける）の過去形
Christmas Eve　クリスマスイブ　a driver's license　自動車運転免許証　drive　ドライブ
steps　step（階段）の複数形　bottom　一番下の　for yourself　自分で　center　中心部
blessed　幸せな

(1)　The following passage（ⅰ）〜（ⅲ）should be put in ⎡　①　⎤ in the order that makes the most sense.（　　　）

　（ⅰ）　Tom also became busy and couldn't spend much time with Paul.

　（ⅱ）　Every year, he gave a wonderful gift to Paul on his birthday.

　（ⅲ）　But he loved Paul very much and always cared about him.

　　　　ア　（ⅰ）→（ⅱ）→（ⅲ）　　イ　（ⅰ）→（ⅲ）→（ⅱ）

　　　　ウ　（ⅱ）→（ⅰ）→（ⅲ）　　エ　（ⅱ）→（ⅲ）→（ⅰ）

(2)　The word which should be put in ⎡　②　⎤ is（　　　）

　ア　on.　　イ　at.　　ウ　as.　　エ　to.

(3)　The word which should be put in ⎡　③　⎤ is（　　　）

　ア　happy.　　イ　sad.　　ウ　right.　　エ　wrong.

(4)　The phrase which should be put in ⎡　④　⎤ is（　　　）

　ア　buy than to give.　　イ　give than to buy.　　ウ　give than to receive.

　エ　receive than to give.

(5)　According to the passage,（　　　）

　ア　when Paul's mother died, his father ran more than ten restaurants.

　イ　Tom gave a Christmas gift to Paul after he got a driver's license.

　ウ　a boy wanted to have a brother like Tom.

　エ　Paul went for a drive with a boy and his younger brother.

Chapter3 *Writing*

1 When you have lunch at school, which do you like better, bento or school lunch? Tell us your opinion and reason. You should write about 50 words.

2 Tell us what you do to protect the environment. You should write about 50 words.

3 What country are you interested in? Tell us why you are interested in this country. You should write about 50 words.

4 In some schools, students can carry their cell phones in school. Do you agree or disagree with carrying cell phones in school? If you agree, begin with "Yes", and if you don't agree, begin with "No", and write your reason. You should write about 50 words.

5 Today there are many 24-hour convenience stores in Japan. Do you think it is good or bad for us? Write your opinion in English with about 50 words.

6 An exchange student from Canada is going to visit your school for two weeks. You are going to tell the student about Japanese national holidays. Which holiday would you like to choose, Children's Day or Respect for the Aged Day? And why? Circle "Children's Day" or "Respect for the Aged Day" and write your reasons after the given English with about 50 English words, not including the given English.

I would like to choose [Children's Day ： Respect for the Aged Day], because

7   Please introduce yourself and tell us about something that is important to you. Please tell us why it is important to you. You should write about 50 words.

8   To become a globally-minded person, what should we learn other than English? You should write about 50 words.

Chapter4 *Listening*

【 Part A 】

No.1 1 (   ) 2 (   ) 3 (   ) 4 (   ) 5 (   ) 6 (   )

1 ア Show the man how to start the computer.

   イ Tell the man to call someone to help him.

   ウ Call someone to help the man.

   エ Start the computer for the man.

2 ア The woman should go to bed early every night.

   イ The woman should stop sleeping.

   ウ The woman should want to do something.

   エ The woman should go home and go to bed.

3 ア He found his cell phone in his pocket.

   イ He lost the woman's cell phone.

   ウ He lost his cell phone on the train.

   エ He asked the woman to find his cell phone.

4 ア Cherry blossoms and roses.

   イ Cookies and cherry blossoms.

   ウ Cookies and roses.

   エ Only roses.

5 ア Happy and excited.

   イ Sad and tired.

   ウ Sorry for the baby.

   エ Surprised at the news.

6 ア Take the woman to Nagano with him.

   イ Introduce the woman to his uncle.

   ウ Grow some vegetables in Nagano.

   エ Send the woman some vegetables.

No.2   1 (   )   2 (   )   3 (   )   4 (   )   5 (   )   6 (   )

1   ア   To the library.

   イ   To the hospital.

   ウ   To the shopping mall.

   エ   To the airport.

2   ア   He feels sad.

   イ   He feels happy.

   ウ   He feels angry.

   エ   He feels nervous.

3   ア   Go to the hospital with the woman.

   イ   Take the woman to the hospital.

   ウ   Take the woman's cat to the station.

   エ   Take the woman's cat to the hospital.

4   ア   Fish and fried chicken.

   イ   Fish and rice.

   ウ   Fried chicken and tomatoes.

   エ   Fish, rice and tomatoes.

5   ア   It's just before six in the evening.

   イ   It's six in the evening.

   ウ   It's just after six in the morning.

   エ   It's six in the morning.

6   ア   To ask her mother to wait.

   イ   To go home to get her cell phone.

   ウ   To borrow the man's cell phone to call her teacher.

   エ   To go to the station to meet her teacher.

【 Part B 】

No.1 (1)(   ) (2)(   )

(1) ア Because she liked math very much.

  イ Because she wanted to become a math teacher.

  ウ Because she wanted some hot milk from her grandfather.

  エ Because she had a lot of math homework.

(2) ア She learned that it's important to try to understand how others feel.

  イ She learned that it's difficult to take care of the dog.

  ウ She learned that it's important to study every night.

  エ She learned that it's difficult to make hot milk.

No.2 (1)(   ) (2)(   )

(1) ア Because he went to school.

  イ Because he got a soccer ball.

  ウ Because he bought a tennis racket.

  エ Because he couldn't come to the festival.

(2) ア They can learn how to get to the park.

  イ They can learn when to use a tennis racket.

  ウ They can learn what to do to help the earth.

  エ They can learn where to have a soccer game.

【 Part C 】

※　音声の指示があるまで英文を読んではいけません。

No.1

The Development of zoos

Probably most of you have visited a zoo. Do you know how zoos have developed?

In 1828, the first modern zoo, London Zoo, was opened in London. It showed many different kinds of animals for studying. After London, many other big cities like Amsterdam and Berlin started to have their own zoos.

At first, animals were kept in cages. But since the 1980s, zoos in America have changed their ways of showing animals to people. In those zoos, animals live in a near-natural environment. Grass, trees, and rocks around the animals are real or look very real. Probably those animals are much happier in the environment like this.

Today, there are many zoos which can give you a chance to get closer to animals. You can not only see the animals but also touch them and give them food. Why don't you visit one of those zoos and study about animals?

（注）　development　発達　　develop　発達する　　modern　近代的な
　　　　Amsterdam　アムステルダム　　Berlin　ベルリン　　cage　おり
　　　　near-natural environment　自然に近い環境　　not only ～ but also …　～だけでなく…も

No.2

How useful are smartphones?

Do you have a smartphone? Probably you have one. Young people often say that they can't live without them. Surely, smartphones are very useful, because if you have one, you can do a lot of things like seeing maps, reading books and magazines, finding train schedules, taking pictures and videos, and sharing them with your friends. Reading books and magazines on the smartphone is cheaper than reading paper books and magazines. And also these digital contents are better for the environment because there is much less waste of paper.

On the other hand, there are some negative points about using smartphones. Students are often so busy talking, sending e-mails, and playing games on their smartphones that they have very little time to study. And spending too much time on the smartphone can hurt our eyes and even affect our sleep.

Smartphones will be more and more useful in the future. And there will be more and more people who can't live without them.

（注）　surely　きっと　　train schedule　電車の時刻表

digital content　デジタル・コンテンツ（コンピュータのコンテンツ）

on the other hand　一方で　　negative　否定的な，悪い

be busy ～ing　～するのに忙しい　　affect　影響を与える

§1．誤文訂正 （4 ページ）

● (1) 「もし〜ならば」という意味の if に続く動詞は，未来を表す場合でも現在形。

(2) news は単数扱いの名詞。

(3) 「〜もまた」を表す語は，否定文では either。

(4) 「うるさくしないで」という命令文。noisy は形容詞なので〈Don't be ＋形容詞〉の形。

(5) 「昨日から」は for ではなく since を用いる。

(6) water は数えられない名詞なので s をつけない。

(7) yesterday があるので，過去形になる。

(8) 〈something ＋形容詞〉の語順になる。something hot ＝「何か熱いもの」。

(9) 主語の one of my friends は単数なので is になる。one of 〜＝「〜の 1 人，1 つ」。

(10) 「トムはそれを知って驚くでしょう」。「〜して驚く」＝ be surprised to 〜。

(11) car は数えられる名詞。数えられる名詞の数をたずねる表現は how many。

(12) reading English books は単数扱い。be 動詞は is。

(13) while は接続詞で，〈主語＋動詞〉が続く。名詞句の前には，前置詞の during をおく。

(14) careful ＝「注意深い」。When she drives a car, Kathy is more careful than her sister. が正しい。

(15) 関係代名詞の先行詞が人と動物（the man in a cap と the dog）なので，who ではなく that を使う。

(16) a friend of me ではなく a friend of mine。

(17) 「レオは全ての科目の中で歴史が一番好きだ」。最上級の文。「〜が一番好きだ」＝ like 〜〔the〕best。

(18) 「彼はたくさんのお金をそれにどのように使わなければならないのかを知っている」。

(19) 「〜された」は過去分詞で表すので drawn が正しい。

(20) 「ハリソン夫妻は 15 年以上前に日本に引っ越してきたアメリカ人です」。

(21) 「あの生徒は家に帰った直後に眠りました」。前置詞のあとは名詞か動名詞が続く。

(22) 主語は The books she read yesterday で，複数形。was written を were written にする。

(23) stop to 〜＝「〜するために立ち止まる」。stop 〜ing は「〜することを止める」という意味。

(24) want A to 〜＝「A に〜してほしい」。

(25) 「私に与えられた時計」。「〜された」と修飾するのは過去分詞。

(26) enjoy の後には不定詞ではなく動名詞が続く。

(27) 「海外へ行く」は go abroad。to は不要。

(28) 「日本食は多くの人々に愛されている」。受動態の文。〈be 動詞＋過去分詞＋ by 〜〉の形にする。

【答】(1) エ　(2) ア　(3) ウ　(4) エ　(5) エ　(6) エ　(7) ア　(8) ウ　(9) ウ　(10) ウ

(11) ア　(12) イ　(13) イ　(14) ウ　(15) ウ　(16) エ　(17) ウ　(18) イ　(19) イ　(20) ウ

(21) エ　(22) ウ　(23) エ　(24) イ　(25) ア　(26) ウ　(27) イ　(28) ア

§２．英文完成（6ページ）

● ⑴ 主語の My friend は 3 人称単数。

⑵ 主語は Judy and Ken で複数。now があるので時制は現在。

⑶ 「今，行っていいですよ」。助動詞 may のあとなので，動詞は原形。

⑷ 「英語は世界中で話されている言語です」。過去分詞 spoken が後ろから the language を修飾する。

⑸ 「あなたはそこで走っている女性を知っていますか？」。running が後ろから the woman を修飾する。

⑹ 「サムはそのニュースを聞いて驚きました」。be surprised ＝「驚く」。主語は Sam で単数。

⑺ Could you tell me the way to ～?＝「～への道を教えてくださいませんか？」。

⑻ 「あなたは宿題をもうしてしまいましたか？」。現在完了〈have/has ＋過去分詞〉の疑問文。

⑼ 「私が帰宅したとき，母は映画を見ていました」。過去進行形の文。

⑽ 「私を手伝ってくれてありがとう」。thank you for ～ing ＝「～してくれてありがとう」。

⑾ 「あなたは雨が降る前に帰宅すべきです」。before ～ ＝「～する前に」。

⑿ 「海で泳ぐことができるので，夏は私の大好きな季節です」。because ～ ＝「～なので」。

⒀ How far is it from ～ to …?＝「～から…へはどのくらいの距離ですか？」。

⒁ by ～ ＝「～（交通手段）で」。

⒂ in English ＝「英語で」。

⒃ 「私たちは月曜日から土曜日まで学校に行きます」。from ～ to … ＝「～から…まで」。

⒄ 「あなたは朝食に何を食べましたか？」。what ＝「何を」。

⒅ 「あなたは私より上手にスキーをすることができます」。than があるので，比較級の文。well - better - best。

⒆ 「鏡で自分を見てください」。look at oneself ＝「自分を見つめる」。

⒇ 「子どもたちが好きな映画がたくさんあります」。ものを先行詞とする関係代名詞を選ぶ。

(21) 「英語を話すことは私にとって難しいのです」。「～すること」を動名詞で表す。speak ～ ＝「～を話す」。

(22) 「この部屋では静かにしなさい」。形容詞の命令文は be で始める。

(23) 「コーヒーはいかがですか？」。

(24) in my family とあるので最上級の文。early ＝「（時間が）早い」。fast ＝「（速度が）速い」。

(25) 「英語を勉強するためにオーストラリアに行きたい」。〈to ＋動詞の原形〉で「～するために」を表す。

(26) salt は数えられない名詞なので複数形にはならず，前に置くのは much である。

(27) every の後には単数形の名詞が続く。visit の後に to は必要ない。

(28) 間接疑問文の語順は〈疑問詞＋主語＋動詞〉。

(29) 「そのネコは私の家族全員にキティと呼ばれています」。受動態の文。by ～ ＝「～によって」。

(30) 「あなたはだれがアメリカを発見したのか知らないですよね？」―「知りません」。

(31) be dying ＝「枯れかけている」。水をやろうとしているのだから，まだ枯れてはいない。

【答】⑴ イ ⑵ ウ ⑶ ア ⑷ ウ ⑸ ア ⑹ エ ⑺ ア ⑻ ウ ⑼ エ ⑽ イ

⑾ イ ⑿ エ ⒀ イ ⒁ ア ⒂ ア ⒃ イ ⒄ エ ⒅ ウ ⒆ ウ ⒇ イ

(21) ア (22) ウ (23) イ (24) エ (25) エ (26) ア (27) ア (28) イ (29) エ (30) エ

(31) ア

§3. 実践問題 (8 ページ)

● (1) 「その女性はその切符の買い方を私に尋ねた」。〈ask ＋ 人 ＋ ～〉＝「人に～を尋ねる」。how to ～ ＝「～する方法」。

(2) 「そのパーティーに行くことができたらいいのになあ」。「～することができたらいいのになあ」＝ I wish I could ～。

(3) 「砂糖は料理を甘くするのに使用される」。〈make ＋ A ＋ ～(形容詞)〉＝「A を～にする」。

(4) 「あの帽子はこの帽子ほど高価ではない」。〈not as ＋ ～(形容詞) ＋ as …〉＝「…ほど～ではない」。ここでの one は主語にある hat を受けている。

(5) 「ユキの両親はよく，彼女に熱心に勉強するように言う」。tell A to ～ ＝「A に～するように言う」。

(6) 「私のかばんを運ぶのを手伝ってくれませんか？」。〈help ＋ A ＋ ～(動詞の原形)〉＝「A が～するのを手伝う」。

(7) 「もしお金がたくさんあったらあなたは何をしますか？」。仮定法の疑問文。〈What would you do if you ＋ ～(動詞の過去形)?〉＝「もし～だったらあなたは何をしますか？」。

(8) 「宿題をしている女の子は私の妹だ」。主格の関係代名詞を用いた文。who が後ろから the girl を修飾する。

(9) 「その数学の問題は，私にとってあまりにも難しすぎたので解けなかった」。too ～ to … ＝「あまりにも～なので…できない」。

(10) 「私は息子におじが私にくれたギターをあげるつもりだ」。〈give ＋ 人 ＋ もの〉＝「人にものを与える」。that は関係代名詞。

(11) 「私の両親は私が高校生のときに私を留学させてくれた」。〈let ＋ A ＋ ～(動詞の原形)〉＝「A に～させる」。

(12) 「あそこに建っている家は約 20 年前に建てられた」。〈名詞 ＋ ～ing〉で「～している名詞」という意味。現在分詞が前の名詞を修飾している。

(13) 「人々が海の中に投げ入れるビニール袋は動物たちにたくさんの深刻な問題をもたらす」。目的格の関係代名詞が省略されているが，people throw into the ocean という部分が plastic bags を修飾している。

(14) 「大阪はさまざまな国から来た多くの人々に訪れられている都市だ」。過去分詞の後置修飾。visited 以下が a city を修飾する。

(15) 「先生は，私たちにとって他人の気持ちを理解しようとすることは本当に必要だと言った」。it is ～ for A to … ＝「A にとって…することは～だ」。

(16) 「それらの科学の教科書はとても難しかったので，私はそれらを理解できなかった」。so ～ that … ＝「とても～なので…」。

(17) 「その夕食パーティーのために，どのような種類の服を着るべきか私に教えていただけませんか？」。間接疑問の疑問詞の後は〈主語 ＋ 動詞〉になることに注意。what kind of ～ ＝「どのような種類の～」。

(18) 「私はチームのみんなに，スミスさんのための歓迎パーティーに参加してほしいと思った」。want A to ～ ＝「A に～してほしいと思う」。

(19) 「何年も前に開店したそのレストランは昨日，別の町に移転した」。The restaurant を先行詞とする主格の関係代名詞 which によって導かれる節を主語に置く。move ＝「移転する」。

(20) 「マリは，おじが自分に本を買ってくれたことをうれしく思った」。形容詞 happy の後ろに that 節が続く形にする。buy A B ＝「A に B を買う」。

(21) 「祖母は 1 年間，公園で育っている植物に水をあげ続けている」。動作の継続を表す現在完了進行形〈have/has been ＋ ～ing〉の文。「～している…」は形容詞的用法の現在分詞で表すことができる。

(22) 「キョウコは，あの料理を作るのにどれくらいの砂糖が必要か知りたいと思った」。know の目的語に間

接疑問文〈疑問詞＋主語＋動詞〉を置く形にする。「どれくらいの砂糖」＝ how much sugar。

【答】(1) ウ　(2) ウ　(3) イ　(4) ウ　(5) エ　(6) エ　(7) イ　(8) ア　(9) ウ　(10) ア

(11) ア　(12) イ　(13) イ　(14) イ　(15) エ　(16) イ　(17) ア　(18) ウ　(19) イ　(20) ア

(21) エ　(22) ウ

Chapter2 Reading　解答・解説

§1．図表を含む問題（10ページ）

1．(1)　However と other people に着目する。Ｄ の前の文で挿入する文と逆接的な内容を述べている。また，some people 〜, other people …で，「〜する人もいるが，…する人もいる」という意味。

(2)　among them は「それらの中で」という意味。them は同文前半の３か国を指している。

【答】(1) エ　(2) イ

2．(1)　「ブラジルでは家族と一緒に時間を過ごすことが最も人気のある活動だ」→「そこ（＝ブラジル）の若者の60 ％以上がそうする」。

(2)　アは「買い物」，イは「本を読むことや音楽を聞くこと」，ウは「テレビを見ること」，エは「友達と一緒に時間を過ごすこと」という意味。直前の文に「日本では買い物が本を読んだり音楽を聞いたりすることよりも人気がある」とあり，後の文に「ブラジルではごく少ない割合だけが休日に買い物に行く」とある。ブラジルでは，買い物は読書や音楽鑑賞ほど人気がないということ。

【答】(1) ウ　(2) ア

3．(1)　Ｃ の直前に「２つの考えがある」と述べられている。"First, 〜" は，いくつかのことを列挙する場合に使う表現。１つ目の考えを First を使って述べ，２つ目の考えを Second を使って述べている。

(2)　直前に「それら（＝木）は空気中の二酸化炭素を減らす」とある。

【答】(1) ウ　(2) イ

4．(1)　受動態〈be 動詞＋過去分詞〉の文。by 〜ing ＝「〜することによって」。「心の健康は朝食を食べることによって保たれる」。朝食が心に及ぼす影響について述べているのは，第３段落。

(2)　アは「朝食を抜く人にはいつも悪いことが起こるだろう」という意味。イは「朝食を抜く人は，考えなければならない時に注意深くできない」という意味。ウは「朝食を抜く人は寝るのが遅く，早起きができない」という意味。エは「朝食を抜く人はテレビやコンピュータの前に座るのが好きだ」という意味。直後の２文に具体的な例があげられている。

【答】(1) ウ　(2) イ

5．(1)挿入する文は「質問は『５月に何冊本を読んだか？』だった」という意味。「約 3,000 人の中学生と約 3,600 人の高校生が回答した」とあるので，その前に質問があるとわかる。Ａ に入るのでアが正解。

(2)the most books は「一番多くの本」，the fewest books は「一番少ない本」。表によると，高校生が一番多くの本を読んだのは 2010 年，一番少なかったのは 2016 年。したがって，ウが正解。

(3)直前の「中学生と高校生が読んだ本の平均の数の合計を見てみよう」に注目する。表によると，一番多かったのは 2010 年の 6.1 冊。

【答】(1) ア　(2) ウ　(3) ア

6．(1)空所を含む文は「私たちは４つのグループ全てで，〜が１位もしくは２位になったということが見て取れる」という意味。表より，４つのグループで１位もしくは２位に選ばれた活動はウォーキングだとわかる。

(2) 空所を含む文は「7つの選択肢の中で，〜は20歳から29歳の女性の間では4位だったが，それは50歳から59歳の男性の間では最下位だった」という意味。グラフより，20歳から29歳の女性の間で4位，50歳から59歳の男性の間で7位に位置しているのは，水泳である。

(3) 空所を含む文は「〜を選んだ人の割合は4つのグループの間で最も大きく異なっていた」という意味で，直後の文に「割合の最大の差異は50以上だった」とある。グラフより，ランニングを選んだ20代男性が62.6％だったのに対し，同じ活動を選んだ50代女性は7.4％で，その差は55.2％である。

【答】(1) ア　(2) イ　(3) イ

§2．短い英文を読む問題① (17ページ)

1. (1) この話は「他の人に伝言を伝えることについて」のものである。
　(2) 第1段落の1文目を見る。筆者は「コミュニケーションは人から人へ考えが伝えられる方法だ」と言っている。
　(3) 直後の文にある how do you tell things to your friend に着目する。何を伝えたいかということ。
　(4) 第3段落の最終文を見る。太鼓を3回たたくことは，「食べ物を見つけた」ということを意味する。
　(5) 第4段落を見る。北アメリカでは，人々は煙を使って考えを伝えていた。

【答】(1) ア　(2) イ　(3) ウ　(4) ア　(5) ウ

2. (1) 第1段落を見る。学校に関する情報を得ることができる。
　(2) 第2段落を見る。手紙をはやく送ることができるようになった。
　(3) 直後の we will need about two weeks に着目する。紙に書く手紙のこと。
　(4) 第3段落の6文目を見る。インターネットを使えば，生徒は家で授業を受けることができる。
　(5) 第4段落の5文目を見る。学校へ行かなければ人間関係を学ぶことができない。

【答】(1) ウ　(2) ア　(3) ア　(4) エ　(5) イ

3. (1) 第2段落を見る。最初の魔法瓶が作られたのは，1世紀以上前。
　(2) 第2段落の最終文を見る。テルモス瓶が世界中でとても一般的であるので，魔法瓶に「テルモス」という名前を使う。
　(3) 最終段落の3文目を見る。空気がないことを意味する。
　(4) 最終段落の最後から2文目を見る。丈夫で軽いのでどこへでも持ち運ぶことができる。
　(5) 最終段落の最終文を見る。テルモス瓶は飲み物を24時間冷たいままに保つ。

【答】(1) ア　(2) ウ　(3) ア　(4) イ　(5) エ

4. (1) サチコはベティの発表を聞いてうれしく思っている。2人は同じクラスの生徒である。
　(2) ブラジルの人はするが日本の人はしないことを選ぶ。
　(3) サチコは勉強を手伝ってくれ，他の人も親切なので，ベティは日本での暮らしを気に入っている。
　(4) ベティの日本での滞在が話題の中心となっているので，「日本でのホームステイ」が適切。

【答】(1) イ　(2) イ　(3) ウ　(4) エ

◀全訳▶　ベティは学生です。ブラジルの出身です。彼女は今，サチコの家族のところに滞在しています。約2か月前に，彼女は日本語を学ぶために日本へやって来ました。ベティとサチコは同じクラスにいます。

　昨日，サトウ先生が生徒たちに言いました。「ええと，私たちはこのクラスにベティのようないい生徒が来てくれて幸せだ。今，きみは日本での自分の生活についてどう考えているかな，ベティ？」

　ベティは立ち上がって言いました。「最初着いたとき，すべてのことが私にとって新しいものでした。今でさえ，とても多くのことが違って見えます。私たちの国では，家で私たちはよく靴をはきますが，あなたがたは違います。ブラジルではクリスマスが夏にやって来ますが，日本では冬にやって来ます。最初，私はう

まく日本語を話すことができませんでした。今，私はそれをとても熱心に勉強しています。サチコが私の勉強を手伝ってくれます。他の人たちもまた私に親切です。今，私はここでの生活をとても楽しんでいます」サチコはそれを聞いて，とても喜びました。

5. (1) 直後の文を見る。イーヤク語を話す人はたった１人しかいない。話し手の数が少ない言語について述べている。

   (2) 「多くの味のカレーがあるのと同様に多くの言語がある」という文脈。「もし 50 キロメートル移動したら」→「異なる言語を耳にする」。

   (3) この段落では，日本にはアイヌ語を話す人や 50 の国から来た外国人がいるということが述べられている。日本では１つの言語しか話されないと言う人もいるが，そうではない。

   (4) 世界の言語について述べている文章。

   【答】(1) ア　(2) イ　(3) ア　(4) イ

◀全訳▶　こんにち，地球上に住んでいる約 60 億人の人々が，約 7,000 の異なった言語を使います。多くの話し手を持つ言語もあります。中国語はそのような言語の１つです。約 9 億人の人々が様々な中国語を話します。ほとんど話し手がいない言語もあります。北アメリカの言語のイーヤク語には，たった１人の話し手しかいません。

　言語の価値は話し手の数ではありません。全ての言語が重要です。それぞれの言語は話し手の心です。

　たった１つの国においてさえ，人々は多くの言語を使います。例えば，インドを例にとってみましょう。ご存じのとおり，インドはそのカレーで有名ですが，カレーの味は 25 キロメートルごとに変化します。このことはインドの言語にもあてはまります。もしあなたが 50 キロメートル移動したら，あなたは異なった言語を耳にするでしょう。インド人は全体で約 350 の言語を話します。それらの中で 18 の言語が公用語です。ですから，あなたはテレビやラジオで少なくとも 18 の言語を聞くことができます。

　日本はどうでしょう？　「日本では１つの言語しか話さない」と言う人々もいます。しかし，そうではありません。北海道ではアイヌ語を話す人々もいます。現在，約 160 万人の外国人が日本に住んでいます。彼らは 50 の異なった国の出身です。

　外国語は私たちの日常生活の中にもあります。大阪では，あるラジオ局から 14 か国語を聞くことができます。東京のような大都市では，複数の言語で書かれた標識を目にします。ですから，日本のいくつかの町を「多言語社会」と呼ぶことができるのです。

6. (1) 次の段落の１文目に「雨が丘の上に降るとき，水は石の小さな cracks と穴の中に流れ落ちる」とある。opening =「隙間，開いている部分」。

   (2) ほとんどの洞窟は，「石灰岩と雨水によって」つくられる。第３段落の１文目を見る。

   (3) 洞窟の中で美しい形をつくるためには，雨水と空気が洞窟の中で石灰岩に触れて溶かすことが必要。

   (4) 洞窟の中で見上げたときは，「stalactites が見える」。第５段落の５文目を見る。

   (5) so ～ that …＝「非常に～なので…」。柱がたくさんあるので教会のように見えるチャンバーもある。

   【答】(1) エ　(2) ア　(3) エ　(4) ウ　(5) イ

◀全訳▶　さまざまな種類の洞くつがあります。何百万年間も存在し続けてきた洞くつもありますが，多くはできてから数千年しかたちません。ほとんどの洞くつはだれかがつくったものでなく自然なものですが，人工的なもの，つまり，人々によってつくられた洞くつもあります。

　小さな部屋よりもさらに小さな洞くつもありますが，何百キロメートルもの長さがあるものもあります。最もおもしろいものには，大小の「部屋」（チャンバーと呼ばれます）がたくさんあり，それらの間には広い道や狭い道がついています。それらには地下の川や滝もあります。

　自然の洞くつのほとんどは，雨水と石灰岩と呼ばれるやわらかい灰色や白色の石によって何千年も前につくられました。石灰岩は２つの点で特別です。第１に，石灰岩はひび割れや穴をたくさん含んでいます。第

2に，雨水や空気が石灰岩に触れると，それらは石灰岩を溶かします。

　雨が丘の上に降るとき，水は石の小さなひび割れと穴の中に流れ落ちます。それは石を溶かし，ゆっくりとひび割れをより広くします。そのあと，水は地面の下をどんどん流れていき，溶けた石灰岩を一緒に運びます。溶けた石灰岩でいっぱいの水のしずくがやわらかい石を通り抜けて下の洞くつに落ちていくこともあります。石灰岩は再び固くなります。ゆっくりと，奇妙で美しい形がたくさんつくられます。

　洞くつの中には，何千年も前に乾いた地下の川を横切る自然の石の橋があるものもあります。石でできた大きな滝があります。木や花のような奇妙な形のものがあります。最も有名な形のものは鍾乳石と石筍です。鍾乳石は洞くつの天井から下りてきます。石筍は床から上ってきます。鍾乳石と石筍が出会うとき，それらは柱をつくります。柱であまりにいっぱいなので，教会のように見えるチャンバーもあります。これらの形のもののほとんどは洞くつの石灰岩と同じ色ですが，いつもそうであるわけではありません。水が金属を含むなら，その形のものは多くのさまざまな色でありうるのです。

7. (1)　them は主語の「東ヨーロッパ出身の何千人というユダヤ人」を指す。
　(2)　ask A to ～ =「A に～するように頼む」。them は「アメリカ兵」を指す。
　(3)　パンケーキについて書かれているのは第2段落。
　(4)　アメリカで人気のある朝食の食べ物の歴史について書かれている。

【答】(1) エ　(2) ア　(3) イ　(4) イ

◀全訳▶　世界中の他の多くの国のように，アメリカでの人気のある朝食の飲食物は，コーヒー，牛乳，ジュース，卵，そしてパンを含みます。アメリカで出されるその他のいくつかの朝食の品目は，伝統的にアメリカのものであると多くの人々に思われています。しかしながら，それらは，実は他の文化に由来するものです。

　アメリカでとても人気のある朝食の食べ物，パンケーキです。小麦粉から作られる薄くて平らなケーキで，しばしばメープルシロップと一緒に出されます。パンケーキという発想は，とても古いものです。実は，パンケーキは古代中国ではるか昔に作られていました。

　真ん中に穴が空いた，丸くて分厚いパンのベーグルもまた，アメリカでは朝食に人気があります。1600年代後期にポーランド人が最初のベーグルを思いつき，この新しい種類のパンはすぐに東ヨーロッパ全体に広がりました。

　1800年代後期には，東ヨーロッパ出身の何千人というユダヤ人がアメリカに旅をして，ベーグルの調理法をもたらしました。今日では，ニューヨークのベーグルは世界で最もおいしいと言われています。多くの人々が出先で朝食にクリームチーズとともにそれらを食べます。

　ドーナツ（ふつうアメリカでは「donut」とつづられる）は，フランスから来ました。第一次世界大戦中のフランスで，それらはアメリカ兵に出されました。戦後，アメリカ兵は，アメリカにいる調理人に自分たちにドーナツを作るように頼みました。今では，コーヒーとともに出され，それらはアメリカ中でとても人気のある朝食の食べ物です。

8. (1)　電話を家に忘れてきたら，電話のために走って戻る。
　(2)　同文の前半を見る。「その装置（＝スマートフォン）がなくなるということ」を指す。
　(3)　「スマートフォンはコミュニケーションのために使われているが，実際には，人々が顔を合わせてコミュニケーションをとることを妨げる壁になっている」ということの具体例は，第4段落に述べられている。
　(4)　スマートフォンの長所と短所の両方が述べられた文章である。

【答】(1) ア　(2) ウ　(3) ウ　(4) エ

◀全訳▶　現在，20代の人々のほとんどがスマートフォンを持っています。彼らは，コミュニケーションの道具としてだけでなく，個人用のコンピュータとしてもスマートフォンを使っています。スマートフォンには，例えば，時計，カレンダー，インターネット，計算機，地図，カメラ，音楽プレーヤーなどの多くの役立つものがあります。朝，家に電話を忘れたら，彼らはしばしばそれらのために走って戻ります。仕事や授業に遅

れることは気にしません。この小さな機械のない生活を想像することは難しいのです。

スマートフォンを使う利点はたくさんあります。今ではインターネットを使うことが簡単なので，若者たちは宿題のための調べものをすばやく簡単にすることができます。このことは，しばしば，10代の若者たちが図書館へ行かなくても，紙の辞書で単語を調べなくても，より多くの情報を手に入れるのに役立ちます。

ナビゲーションソフトを使えば，以前に行ったことのない場所をより簡単に見つけることができます。そのうえ，ソーシャルネットワーキングサービスのおかげで，いつでも，どこでも，世界中の友達や家族とコミュニケーションをとることができます。実際，新しいスマートフォンソフトが毎日作られていて，この小さな装置はさらにより役立つようになり得ます。

一方では，否定的な点がいくつかあります。毎日オンラインゲームをしてかなり多くの時間を浪費する子どもたちがいます。彼らはもっと外での活動をし，宿題をすべきです。いくつかの家庭では，家族が夕食の席でもスマートフォンを使うので，お互いに話をしません。何が起こっているのかわかりますか？　スマートフォンはコミュニケーションのために使われていますが，実際には，人々が顔を合わせてコミュニケーションをとることを妨げる壁になっているのです。

スマートフォンの中には多くの個人情報があります。もし装置がなくなったら，重大な問題になる場合があるでしょう。その個人情報のすべてが他のだれかに盗まれるという危険があるかもしれません。これはおそろしくないですか？

私たちは現在，科学技術の世界に暮らしています。スマートフォンは日常生活でとても役立つとても便利なものなので，それらなしでは生活することができません。しかし，私たちは慎重になり，これらの装置を賢く使うべきなのです。

§3．短い英文を読む問題② (28 ページ)

1．(1) 設問文は「本文によると，ユネスコは無形文化遺産のリストを作成している，なぜなら～からだ」という意味。アは「彼らは西洋の文化を尊重することが大事だと思った」，イは「彼らはそれらを見たり触れたりしたいと思った」，ウは「彼らは世界の文化を十分によく知っている人々を尊敬している」，エは「彼らは世界中のさまざまな重要な文化を保護したいと思った」という意味。第1段落2・3文目の内容に合うエが正解。

(2) 下線部①の指している内容を答える問題。アは「2019年に文化的に重要な人々を含んだリスト」，イは「2019年に初めて発見された技術や習慣」，ウは「2019年にリストに追加されたもの」，エは「2019年にリストを作成した国々」という意味。直前の文に「2019年には，55か国における42のものがリストに追加された」とあることから，下線部を含む文では，2019年に無形文化遺産のリストに追加されたものの一例としてタイマッサージに言及しているのだとわかる。よって，ウが正解。

(3) ②を含む文は「その伝統的な祭りは毎年冬に開かれ，それは3日以上～」という意味。文意に合う動詞は，イの continues（続く）。アは「終わる」，ウは「反応する」，エは「見える」という意味。

(4)「本文によると，ボデンセの祭りの間，」に続くものを選ぶ。アは「人々は人形を燃やしたあと，たくさん踊る」，イは「カラフルな服を着た人々が村を通って歩く」，ウは「人々は必要なものを火の中に投げる」，エは「人々は自分たちの中にいる悪魔を見つけるために，互いにあいさつする」という意味。第4段落1文目の内容を言い換えたイが正解。in ～ =「～を着て，～を身につけて」。

【答】(1) エ　(2) ウ　(3) イ　(4) イ

◀全訳▶　文化遺産は私たちが実際に見たり触れたりできるものに限りません。それには，文化的に重要な地域の知識，技術，習慣も含まれます。そのような無形文化遺産を保護し尊重するため，ユネスコはそれらのリストを作成しています。2019年には，55か国における42のものがリストに追加されました。

伝統的なタイマッサージはそのうちの一つです。それはその国における健康のための芸術，科学，伝統的な知識の文化の一部として知られています。セラピストが良いストレッチを施し，そのあとあなたは本当にリラックスすることができます。それは世界中で人気があり，ここ日本でもセラピストが見つかります。

もう一つの例はポルトガルのポデンセ村における地元の祭りです。それも 2019 年にリストに追加されました。その伝統的な祭りは毎年冬に開かれ，3 日以上続きます。男性，女性，子どもたちが，冬の終わりと春の始まりにそれを楽しみます。

祭りの間には，マスクや，鈴のついたカラフルな衣装を着用した人々が，村を練り歩きます。彼らは，自分たちの友人や隣人の家の周りで踊ったり歩き回ることもあります。しかし，その祭りを知るたくさんの人は，最も興奮する瞬間の一つは悪魔のように見える人形を燃やすことだということで，おそらく意見が一致するでしょう。それは，火を通じて悪いものを浄化するプロセスなのです。

2. (1) 下線部①の指している内容を答える問題。アは「私たちが眠っている間に見る，大半の夢」，イは「一晩に複数の夢を見る，大半の人々」，ウは「私たちが眠たいときにすることができる，いくつかのこと」，エは「自分の夢をよく思い出すことができる人々」という意味。ここでの they は直前で述べられている Most dreams（大半の夢）を指しているのでアが正解。

(2)「本文によると，」に続く内容として適切なものを選ぶ。アは「パイロットはしばしば眠っている間に夢の中で飛ぶ」，イは「明晰夢を研究することには良い面と悪い面がある」，ウは「明晰夢はいくつかの人々にとって研究テーマであり続けている」，エは「コーヒーを飲むことは夢を思い出すのに役立つ」という意味。第 2 段落 3・4 文目の内容に合うウが正解。

(3)「将来，」に続くものを選ぶ。アは「明晰夢はみんなの記憶から忘れ去られるかもしれない」，イは「いくつかの研究グループが明晰夢の悪い面に特化するだろう」，ウは「人々の 25 パーセントが明晰夢を見られるようになるだろう」，エは「私たちは悪夢を見るのを止め，それらを制御できるようになるかもしれない」という意味。第 3 段落 3～5 文目の内容に合うエが正解。

(4)「本文によると，明晰夢の経験についての報告はたくさんある，」に続く内容として適切なものを選ぶ。アは「しかしアジアの多くの人々は，何世紀もの間それらが何であるか知らなかった」，イは「そして初期のものは古い文化に見つけられる」，ウは「そして古代ギリシャの医者は悪夢を回避させることができた」，エは「しかし科学者たちはそれらの大半が真実の報告ではないとわかっている」という意味。第 4 段落 2・3 文目の内容に合うイが正解。イの ones は設問文にある reports（報告）を受けている。

【答】(1) ア　(2) ウ　(3) エ　(4) イ

◀全訳▶　私たちは皆，誰もが眠っている間に夢を見るということを知っています。また，目覚めたあとで夢を思い出すのが難しいということも，私たちは知っています。大半の夢はすぐに忘れ去られ，それらは水中の小さな泡のように消えます。加えて，それらはしばしば，忘れ去られたあとではまったく思い出されることができません。たとえそれらから目覚めてすぐにある夢を思い出せたとしても，コーヒーを作るためにベッドから出たあとには，もはやそれを思い出すことができないのです。おそらくあなたにもそのような経験があるかもしれませんね。

それでは，あなたは眠っている間に自分が夢を見ているということに気がついたことは今までにありますか？　そのような経験をしたことのある人もいるのです。それは明晰夢（めいせきむ）と呼ばれ，世界中の科学者の中にはその研究を行っている人もいます。実際，それに特化した研究グループさえあります。

彼らはなぜ明晰夢の研究を行っているのでしょうか？　一つには，私たちにとって利点があるかもしれないからです。もし自分が夢を見ていると気がつくことができ，パイロットのようにそれらを制御することができれば，私たちは悪夢を避けて自分の夢をもっと楽しく，あるいはもっとわくわくするようなものにすることができるでしょう。今日，科学者たちは明晰夢とその制御方法について十分にわかっていないので，研究でなされるべきことはまだたくさんあります。しかし，その分野の科学がもっと進歩すれば，誰もが明晰

夢を見ることが可能になるかもしれません。実際それが，何人かの科学者たちが達成しようとしている目標の一つです。

　　ある調査によると，回答者のうち 75 パーセント以上が少なくとも人生で一度は明晰夢を経験したと回答しました。また，歴史上では，明晰夢の経験に関する多くの報告がされています。それに関する初期の報告は古代文化の書物に見られます。例えば，ある古代ギリシャの医者はすでに 2,000 年以上前に，ある種の治療として明晰夢の利用を試みました。それから，自分なりに自分の夢を制御することは，アジアにおける初期の仏教徒の間で重要なテーマの一つだったのです。

3．⑴「電気ウナギは驚くべき，かつ危険な種であり，彼らは」に続く内容として適切なものを選ぶ。アは「ウナギとは違うグループに属し，料理されることができない」，イは「最近まで水族館で見つからなかった」，ウは「数時間，水なしで生きることができる」，エは「捕まえるのが難しいが，それらの味はとてもよい」という意味。第 1 段落 4・5 文目の内容に合うアが正解。

　　⑵①を含む文は「しかし，電気ウナギの最も驚くべき特徴は，約 600 ボルトの電気を〜によって他の動物に電気ショックを与えることができるという事実だ」という意味。文意に合う動名詞は，イの producing（生み出すこと）。アは「食べること」，ウは「受け入れること」，エは「拒否すること」という意味。

　　⑶本文中の②に入る疑問文として適切なものを選ぶ。アは「電気ウナギは世界に何匹いるのだろうか」，イは「動物には何ボルトの電気が危険なのだろうか」，ウは「この電気はどこからくるのだろうか」，エは「電気ウナギはどこで生まれるのだろうか」という意味。直後の文に「それは彼らの体中にある何千もの筋肉細胞から生み出されると言われている」とあり，続けて，電気ウナギの筋肉細胞が生み出す電気について詳しく説明されている。よって，②に入る問いかけとして適切なのはウ。come from 〜＝「〜からくる，〜に由来する」。

　　⑷「本文によると，」に続く内容として適切なものを選ぶ。アは「電気ウナギは水中でもはっきりとものを見たり聞いたりすることができる」，イは「電気ウナギは何かを食べることに決める際，2 種類の電気を使用する」，ウは「ニホンウナギも弱い種類の電気を生み出すことができると知られている」，エは「ニホンウナギは電気ウナギに食べられることがあると言われている」という意味。第 4 段落の内容をまとめたイが正解。decide to 〜＝「〜することに決める」。

【答】⑴ ア　⑵ イ　⑶ ウ　⑷ イ

◀全訳▶　さまざまな動物種の中でも，電気ウナギはおそらく最も驚くべき，かつ危険なものとして知られています。彼らは南アメリカの川に生息しています。あなたはテレビやインターネットの動画，あるいは水族館で彼らを見たことがあるかもしれません。あなたがこれまでに彼らを見たことがあれば，その名前に「ウナギ」という単語が含まれるにもかかわらず，彼らはウナギとはかなり違うということを知っているでしょう。実際，彼らは「ナイフフィッシュ」と呼ばれるグループに分類されており，ウナギのようには食べられません。

　　電気ウナギは長さ 250 センチメートルまで成長できます。ニホンウナギの一般的な長さが約 40 センチメートルであるという事実を考慮すると，電気ウナギはかなり長い動物だとわかります。しかし，電気ウナギの最も驚くべき特徴は，約 600 ボルトの電気を生み出すことで他の動物に電気ショックを与えることができるという事実です。それは，それらを殺すのに十分なほど強力です。参考までに，日本の大半のコンセントは 100 ボルト用です。テレビのリモコンに使用する乾電池は，1.5 ボルトの電気を生み出します。彼らの攻撃がどれだけ強力なものであるか，想像がつくでしょう。

　　その攻撃は一瞬しか続きませんが，非常に強力です。しかし，そもそもこの電気はどこからくるのでしょうか？　それは，彼らの体中にある何千もの筋肉細胞から生み出されると言われています。各筋肉細胞は約 0.15 ボルトの電気しか生み出しません。しかし，何千ものそれらが一斉に働けば，900 ボルトの電気にさえ達することができます。

　　また，電気ウナギは別の種類の電気を使うことができるとも言われています。それはより弱いのですが，

彼らにはそれがディナーのために必要です。彼らはあまりものを見ることができないので，まず弱い種類の電気を使って小さな魚のような食べ物を探します。ターゲットを見つけたあと，彼らの攻撃が始まります。彼らは強い種類の電気を使って食べ物を「料理」し，それを食べるのを楽しむのです。

4．(1) ①を含む文は「それを～した人々は，それが飲むためのカップだと考えた」という意味。直後にある it と that 節中の it が指しているのは，直前の文にある The conch shell。よって，文意に合う動詞はウの discovered（～を発見した）。アは「～を浪費した」，イは「～を支持した」，エは「～を保護した」という意味。

(2) ②を含む文は「2021 年のフランスの研究によれば，そのほら貝はホルンのような楽器～演奏されていた」という意味。文意に合う前置詞はイの as（～として）。

(3)「研究者グループは自分たちの仮説を裏づけたいと思ったので，」に続く内容として適切なものを選ぶ。アは「フランス人科学者は有名な音楽家からホルンのレッスンを受けた」，イは「彼らは音楽家にその大きなほら貝を演奏するよう依頼した」，ウは「彼らは自分たちの研究を手伝ってくれるボランティアを探した」，エは「彼らは楽器を比較するためにホルンを購入した」という意味。第 2 段落の 3・4 文目の内容に合うイが正解。

(4)「本文によると，」に続く内容として適切なものを選ぶ。アは「ほら貝の両端に施された変更にはおそらく目的があった」，イは「ほら貝の内部の赤い点のような模様と穴は，それが 20 世紀にフランスの博物館に渡されてから加えられた」，ウは「約 18,000 年前にフランスの洞窟に暮らしていた人々は，食べたいと思う固い物を切るのにほら貝を使用していた」，エは「最初，ほら貝はおそらく人々が昔何かを飲む際に使われたが，その使い方は後に変えられた」という意味。第 3 段落の 2～6 文目と第 4 段落の 1 文目の内容に合うアが正解。

【答】(1) ウ　(2) イ　(3) イ　(4) ア

◀全訳▶　1931 年に，大きなほら貝がフランスの洞窟で発見されました。その洞窟は古い壁画で有名です。それは山の中にあり，海には近くありません——洞窟から最も近い海は 200 キロメートル以上離れています。そのほら貝は，長さが約 30 センチメートルでした。それを発見した人々は，それが飲むためのカップだと考えました。それは後にフランスの博物館に渡され，人々は最近までそれにほとんど注意を払っていませんでした。

　2021 年のフランスの研究によれば，そのほら貝はホルンのような楽器として演奏されていました。最新技術のおかげで彼らは，このほら貝が飲むためのカップではなく，実際には楽器であることがわかりました。その仮説を裏づけるため，ホルン奏者が研究グループに招かれました。彼らはその音楽家にほら貝を鳴らすよう依頼し，それは 3 つのはっきりした音を鳴らしました。

　研究はそのほら貝が約 18,000 年前のものであるということを示しており，それについて興味深い点が 3 つあります。第一に，ほら貝の一方の端には穴がありました。研究に参加した科学者は，その穴はほら貝の最も固い部分にあるために，これはおそらく意図的なものだろうと言いました。おそらく，誰かが鳴らす目的でそれにマウスピースのようなものを入れるために穴を開けたのです。第二に，もう一方の端には切断された部分がありました。これらの部分は，人々が貝に自分の手を入れて音を簡単に変化させるのを助けることができます。最後に，ほら貝の内部には点のような赤い模様がありました。この模様は洞窟内の絵のそれと類似しています。

　これら 3 つの点は，ほら貝がある理由で人間によって加工されたということを示しています。これはおそらく，その音を改善するため，あるいは儀式の間にそれを楽器として演奏するためでした。この古い楽器は私たちに，人間ははるか昔に音楽を楽しんでいたのだということを教えてくれます。

5．(1) ①を含む文は「中国の人々は伝統的に大きな丸いテーブルの周りに一緒に座って食べ物を～する」という意味。直後に「彼らはたいてい同じ皿から食べ物を取る」とあることから，文意に合う動詞はウの share

（～をシェアする，～を共有する）。

(2)「韓国では銀でできた箸が昔使われていた，なぜなら～」に続く内容として適切なものを選ぶ。アは「そのぴかぴかの表面は鏡として使用可能だった（から）」，イは「銀は他のどの素材よりも高価だった（から）」，ウは「韓国と中国の王はその色を好んでいた（から）」，エは「人々は食べ物の中にある毒を見つけるためにそれを用いることができると考えた（から）」という意味。第3段落の4文目の内容に合うエが正解。

(3) 挿入文は「加えて，それらを何度も洗うのは簡単だ」という意味で，追加を表す In addition（加えて）から始まっていることに着目する。Cの直前に「鋼の箸は表面がぴかぴかで鏡のようなので人気がある」と，鋼の箸についての肯定的な記述がある。挿入文は「洗うのが簡単である」というメリットについて述べた文なので，Cに入れると，挿入文中の them が steel chopsticks を指し，鋼の箸についての肯定的な情報を付け加える流れとなり，文脈として自然。

(4) 4つの文章を適切な順に並べ替えて空所に入れる問題。（ⅰ）は「それでは，日本の箸はなぜ先が尖っているのだろうか？ それらは魚を食べるのに便利なため，先が尖っている。これらの箸は骨を取り除くのを助けてくれる」，（ⅱ）は「この理由は日本の食習慣に見つけることができる。日本人は伝統的に同じ皿の上の食べ物をシェアしないので，日本の箸は短いのだ」，（ⅲ）は「その形のおかげで，私たちは安全に魚を食べることができる。日本の箸のもう1つの興味深い特徴は，その表面だ」，（ⅳ）は「日本の箸は短くて軽い。また，それらは先が尖っている」という意味。まず，空所の直前に「日本の箸はどうだろうか？」とあることから，これに続く文章として適切なのは，日本の箸の2つの特徴（①短い，②先が尖っている）の概要を述べている（ⅳ）だとわかる。次に，（ⅳ）の直後には，①の特徴の理由を説明している（ⅱ）が適切。そして，（ⅱ）の直後には，別の特徴である②に言及している（ⅰ）が適切。最後に，（ⅰ）の直後には，②の特徴のメリット，およびさらに別の特徴について述べている（ⅲ）を続けると，空所の前後を含めた部分の意味が通る。

【答】(1) ウ　(2) エ　(3) ウ　(4) イ

◀全訳▶ 箸は中国，韓国，そして日本で使用されています。これら3つの国で使用されている箸は異なっており，それぞれに独自の特徴があります。

中国の箸は長くて太く，その先が尖っていません。中国の人々は伝統的に，大きな丸いテーブルの周りに一緒に座って食べ物をシェアします。彼らはたいてい同じ皿から食べ物を取るので，彼らにとって長くて太い箸を使うことは便利なのです。

韓国の人々が普段使う箸は重くて丈夫です。その理由は材料に見いだせます。昔は，銀で作られた箸が韓国と中国の王によって使用されていました。人々は，銀の箸を使用して色の変化を見ることで食べ物の中にある毒を見つけることができると信じていました。今日，韓国で使用されている箸の大半はステンレス鋼でできています。鋼の箸は表面がぴかぴかで鏡のようなので，人気があります。さらに，それらを何度も洗うのは簡単なのです。韓国の人々はスプーンで米を食べるため，韓国では，箸はたいていテーブルの上にスプーンと一緒に置かれています。

日本の箸はどうでしょうか？ 日本の箸は短くて軽いです。また，それらは先が尖っています。私たちはこの理由を日本の食習慣に見つけることができます。日本の人々は伝統的に同じ皿の上の食べ物をシェアしないので，日本の箸は短いのです。それでは，日本の箸はなぜ先が尖っているのでしょうか？ それらは魚を食べるのに便利なため，先が尖っているのです。これらの箸は私たちがその骨を取り除くのを助けます。その形のおかげで，私たちは安全に魚を食べることができます。日本の箸のもう1つの興味深い特徴は，その表面です。それらにはたいてい漆が塗られているので長持ちし，多くの人々がその美しさの真価を認めています。そのため，それらはよく，特に日本の外で暮らす人々向けの贈り物として選ばれています。

6. (1) 下線部①の指す単語を答える問題。下線部を含む文で述べられている，「自分たちの作業のうちいくつかを自動式のものにする」と「作物に関する情報をもっと簡単に得て共有する」という行為の主体を考える

と，第1段落の1・2文目にある farmers（農業従事者）を指しているとわかる。

(2) ②を含む文は「それ（自動トラクター）には，車両の前にあるものを見つけることのできるセンサーがついているので，使用するのが〜だ」という意味。理由を表す so までの内容を考えると，文意に合う動詞はアの safe（安全な）。

(3) ③を含む文は「さらに，操縦者なしで果物や野菜を〜することができる機械がある」という意味。空所の後ろにある fruits and vegetables を目的語とする動詞として文意に合うのは，エの「〜を収集する」。

(4)「本文中にある推定によると，」に続く内容として適切なものを選ぶ。アは「草を刈るのに現在使用されている機械を人々が発明するのには75時間以上かかった」，イは「農業に従事する人々は，機械を用いることでより早く草刈りを終えることができる」，ウは「150を超える農業従事者に役立つ機械が，近い将来に開発されるだろう」，エは「2021年4月時点で，日本における200を超える農業地区が最新技術を使用している」という意味。第2段落の6文目の内容に合うイが正解。

【答】 (1) ウ　(2) ア　(3) エ　(4) イ

◀全訳▶　日本では農業従事者の数が減っています。その理由の1つが，農業従事者が毎日しなければならない作業が大変で，時として危険であるということです。トラクターの運転といった仕事は，特別なスキルや経験を必要とします。しかし，この状況は「スマート農業」によって改善され得ます。これは，農業で機械，人工知能，装置といった最新技術を使用することを意味します。それを使用することで，彼らは自分たちの作業のいくつかを自動的にしたり，作物に関する情報をもっと簡単に得たり共有したりすることができます。

　その一例は自動トラクターです。このトラクターは運転手を必要としません。それには車両の前にあるものを見つけることのできるセンサーがついているので，使用するのが安全です。もう一例は，草を刈ることができる機械です。それも自動式かつ小型で，操縦者を必要としません。ある推定によると，その機械を使用することで，草刈りに225時間を必要とする人は同じ作業を75時間で行うことができます。さらに，操縦者なしに果物や野菜を収集することができる機械もあります。

　日本では，スマート農業がどれだけ役に立つかを見極めるため，2019年にあるプロジェクトが始動されました。このプロジェクトにおいて，最新技術が日本の179の農業地区で使用されています（2021年4月時点）。スマート農業の使用のやり方は地域ごとに異なります。例えば，近畿地方では，スマート農業は7つの地区で果樹生産のために使用されているのに対し，それは北陸地方では，同じ目的では1つの地区でしか使用されていません。北陸地方では，スマート農業は畑作や動物の飼育に使用されており，水田作には約10の農業地区で使用されています。それは，園芸や花の栽培にも使用されています。

　スマート農業にはコストやインフラといった困難があることは事実です。しかし，それは近い将来には発展し，農業のやり方を変えるでしょう。

§4．長い英文を読む問題 (37 ページ)

1. (1) プケコとタカへの違いについて述べていることから考える。同文の前半で「プケコは敵から空へ逃げることができる」と述べ，接続詞 but が続いているので，「『タカへ』はできない」という内容になる。

(2) プケコの数が増えていることで，他の鳥たちのすむ場所がなくなっていることについて述べていることから考える。「十分な場所がないため，より小さな鳥たちは『プケコ』の近くにすむことができない」という内容になる。

(3) 第4段落の2文目の「プケコがタカへととても似た色をしており，ボランティアたちはその2種類の鳥を理解していなかった」という文から考える。ハンターたちは自分たちが撃った鳥がタカへであるとは思っていなかった。

(4) 第6段落の4文目を見る。ニュージーランドにはタカへを食べる大型動物がおらず，地上は安全だった

ので，飛ぶ必要がなかったタカへの翼は短いのだとわかる。

(5) ア．「私たちはニュージーランドの道ばたで簡単にプケコを見ることができる」。第１段落の２・３文目を見る。正しい。イ．第４段落の１文目を見る。タカへを殺したのはレンジャーではなく鹿狩りをするハンターである。ウ．第６段落の６文目と第７段落の４文目を見る。タカへは昆虫を食べることもあるが，プケコは菜食者であるとしか述べられていない。エ．最終段落の１文目を見る。タカへもプケコもどちらもニュージーランド原産の鳥である。

【答】(1) ウ　(2) イ　(3) イ　(4) ウ　(5) ア

◀全訳▶　プケコの猟をしていると思っていたハンターにより，絶滅の危機にさらされている鳥の４羽が野鳥の生息地域で殺されたことが新聞に載っていました。プケコはニュージーランドのあらゆる場所にすんでいます。プケコはニュージーランド中の道ばたや野原でとても簡単に見ることができます。

公園管理のために働いているレンジャーは，数人のハンターがニュージーランドで絶滅の危機にさらされている鳥である４羽のタカへを銃で撃ったと述べました。そのハンターたちは絶滅の危機にさらされている鳥のための野鳥生息地域にすんでいるプケコを600羽殺していました。

絶滅の危機にさらされている鳥たちを安全な場所に移すことに同意していたため，その大きな過ちはニュージーランドの人々を怒らせています。

それらのタカへは地元で鹿狩りをするハンターのグループのメンバーによって殺されました。メンバーの１人は，プケコがタカへととても似た色をしており，ボランティアたちはその２種類の鳥を理解していなかったのだと述べました。どちらもおよそ体長が50センチほどです。

しかし，その島で数年前に１羽のタカへが殺されるという類似の事故が起こったあとに，ハンターたちは２種類の鳥の違いについて伝えられていたのです。その死はボランティアにとってもレンジャーにとっても大変悲しいことでした。そこで彼らは長い話し合いを行いました。現在，ニュージーランドにはたった300羽のタカへしかおらず，タカへは「絶滅の危機にさらされている鳥」として知られています。

タカへは飛ぶことができない鳥です。彼らの翼は短すぎて飛ぶことができません。どうしてタカへはニュージーランドで生きることができるのでしょうか？　何年も前には，タカへを食べ物として食べることのできる大型動物がいなかったため，地上にいることは安全だったのです。彼らの大好きな食べ物は植物の葉や，雑草や，種です。彼らは昆虫を食べることもあります。彼らは飛ぶ必要のない鳥になりました。しかし，人間が他の国々から海を渡ってやって来ると，大きな問題が起きました。人々がそこに連れて来た動物たちが彼らを殺して食べ，彼らの食べ物を奪ったのです。タカへの数は減り続けています。絶滅からタカへを守るため，ニュージーランドの人々はタカへを保護しようとしています。彼らはいつも食べ物としてタカへを殺すオコジョや，いつも大量の植物の葉を食べる鹿を駆除してきました。彼らはタカへが産んだ卵を保護して育てています。成長すると，彼らは大人のタカへを草原に戻します。彼らはタカへのための環境を保護しています。

プケコはニュージーランドで最も一般的に見られる鳥の１種です。彼らは国内のどこの道ばたでも見かけられます。彼らはタカへと似ているので，どちらがプケコでどちらがタカへであるのかを知るのは困難です。どちらの鳥も体長が約50センチで，菜食者です。彼らの顔はとてもよく似ています。しかし違いの１つは色です。プケコが濃い青色であるのに対して，タカへはプケコよりも明るい青色です。もう１つの違いは，プケコが飛べるということです。これは大きな違いです。プケコは敵から空へ逃げることができるのですが，タカへにはそれができません。

プケコはニュージーランドにとって頭痛の種となっています。数が増えているため，プケコは他の鳥が暮らしたがっているより多くの草原で暮らしているのです。十分な場所がないため，より小さな鳥たちはプケコの近くにすむことができません。

タカへもプケコもニュージーランド原産の鳥です。人々は彼らを保護したいと思っています。どのようにすればタカへとプケコを助けることができるのでしょうか？

2. (1) 直前に「それら（ロボット）は人間のように見える必要はない」とあることに着目する。第2段落にも，さまざまな形のロボットの例が挙げられていることから「ほとんどのロボットは人間のようには見えない」が入る。

(2) 光を認識するのに私たちに目があるように，ロボットにも光センサーとカメラがあると述べているので，目の働きを考えると「見る」が入る。

(3) どのように振る舞い，どのように動くかを自分で決めることができるので，人はオートノミーを持っているのに対して，テレビや洗濯機は決定をする人に依存するので，「オートノミーを持たない」と考えられる。

(4) オートノミーを持つ自動車ができることについて述べた最終段落に着目する。「地図の中の状況を注意深く検討することができる」が最終段落の3文目以降の内容と合っている。「検討する」＝ study。

(5) ア．第2段落の最終文を見る。人と意思伝達をすることができるロボットは，顔や目や口を持っている。イ．第3段落を見る。ほとんどのロボットはセンサーと作動装置とプログラムを持っているが，家にある他の電化製品はそれらがない。ウ．「人が持つオートノミーは，ロボットが持つオートノミーとは少し異なる」。第8段落を見る。正しい。エ．第9・10段落を見る。全て自分で音楽に合わせて踊ることができるロボットを作るには，コンピューターも必要である。

【答】(1) イ　(2) ア　(3) イ　(4) エ　(5) ウ

◀全訳▶　ロボットのことを考えるとき，あなたは何を想像しますか？　あなたや私に少し似た機械ですか？　実際，ロボットはさまざまな形や大きさをしています。それらは人間のように見える必要はなく，実際にはほとんどのロボットは人間のようには見えません。

ロボットはさまざまな目的のために作られているので，それぞれ異なって見えます。飛ぶロボットはヘリコプターのように見えるかもしれませんし，あるいは昆虫や鳥のように羽があるかもしれません。掃除ロボットはしばしば小さな掃除機のように見えます。人と意思伝達をするために作られたロボットは，ちょうど私たちのように，しばしば顔や目や口を持っています！

ほとんどのロボットはセンサーと作動装置とプログラムという3つの重要な部位を持っています。これら3つの部位が一緒になって，ロボットをコンピューターや洗濯機やテレビのような，家にある他の電化製品とは異なるものにしています。

第1に，ロボットはまわりの世界を認識するのを助けるセンサーを持っています。光を認識する目や，音を認識する耳，触れているものを認識する肌の中の神経を私たちが持っているのとちょうど同じように，ロボットはまわりのものを「見る」ことができるように光センサーとカメラを，「聞く」ことができるようにマイクを，「感じる」ことができるように圧力センサーを持っています。

第2に，ロボットは動きまわるための作動装置を持っています。私たちは歩いたり走ったりするために脚と足を使い，ボールを拾い上げて投げるために手を使います。ロボットはモーターや車輪や，指のように見える部位のような作動装置を使い，それによって，走りまわったり動きまわったり，ものを持ったり制御したり，それらをまわしたりすることができるのです。

第3に，何かを認識したときに，ロボットには行動したり次のことを行ったりするために従うべきプログラムが必要です。自分自身で行動するためのこの能力はオートノミーと呼ばれます。このオートノミーの考え方を見てみましょう。

オートノミーを持つ何かを思い浮かべることはできますか？　人々はほとんどの時間，どのように振る舞い，どのように動くかを自分で決めることができるので，オートノミーを持っています。テレビや洗濯機は決定をする人に依存するので，オートノミーを持たない機械の例です。

ロボットがオートノミーを持つとき，人がロボットに何をすればよいかを伝えるコンピュータープログラムを書かなければいけないので，それは人が持つオートノミーとは少し異なります。たとえば，私たちが音楽を聞くとき，私たちの脳は音楽に合わせてどのように自分の脚を動かせばよいかを伝えるのであり，私た

ちは私たちのために脚を動かしてくれる誰かを必要とはしないのです！

　しかし，全て自分で音楽に合わせて踊ることができるロボットを作りたければ，どんな３つのことが必要でしょうか？　私たちは，踊るためのセンサーと作動装置とプログラムが必要です。

　全ての情報を認識することができ，プログラムを動かすことができるロボットの脳であるコンピューター，そして，ロボットに電気を与えるためのある種のバッテリーも必要となります。

　たくさんのさまざまなことができるロボットもいます。たとえば，オートノミーを持つ自動車はよいセンサーを持っているので，それらのまわりにある全てのものまでどのくらいの距離があるかを見つけ，その区域の三次元の地図を作ることができます。そして，それらは地図中の状況，そこに自動車は何台いるのか？　三次元の地図中の道路や他のものはどこにあるのか？　といったことを理解する優れたプログラムも持っています。それが状況を注意深く理解すると，そのプログラムはロボットの速さと動きを制御するのです。

3. (1)　一言語だけを用いる英英辞書について述べた文である。英語の単語は翻訳されず，「英語」で説明されている。

(2)　空欄の直後に「全ての説明が英語なので」と続いていることから，その直前には一言語だけを用いる英英辞書を使うときのことを述べた文が入るとわかり，最後が（ⅰ）になる。（ⅲ）の文頭の It は「日本語の説明を見るだけであること」を指しているので，（ⅲ）の前に（ⅱ）が入る。「英和辞書を使うときには，私たちの多くは日本語の説明を見るだけである」→「それは速いけれど，多くの場合，日本語の説明を見るだけでは英語を学ぶ助けにはならない」→「一言語だけを用いる辞書を使えば，英語で書かれた説明と例文を何度も読まなければならないだろう」という順になる。

(3)　前文と同文の前半に着目する。excavate を英英辞書で調べたとき dig carefully to find ancient things という説明があり，その説明の中に出てきた知らない単語のことを指している。

(4)　第４段落の１文目に「英英辞書は『簡単な』英語で単語を説明している」とあることに着目する。

(5)　ア．「辞書と考えると，多くの人は二言語を用いる辞書を想像する」。第１段落の３文目を見る。正しい。イ．第１段落の４文目を見る。和英辞書は二言語を用いる辞書である。ウ．第３段落を見る。一言語だけを用いる辞書の方が，説明の中にある知らない単語を再び調べることになるので，英語を向上させる多くの機会を与える。エ．第４段落の３文目を見る。一言語だけを用いる英英辞書の最後の部分に，選んだ単語のリストを見つけることができる。

【答】(1) イ　(2) エ　(3) ウ　(4) ウ　(5) ア

◀全訳▶　英語の辞書は，英語を学ぶときに使うであろう最も重要なものの１つです。よい辞書は，何百もの新しい単語とそれらの使い方を学ぶ助けとなるでしょう。辞書と考えると，たいていは，二言語を用いる辞書を想像します。二言語を用いる辞書とは，英和辞書や和英辞書のような２つの言語の辞書です。英和辞書では，英語の単語は日本語で説明され，和英辞書では，日本語の単語は英語で説明されます。これらは私たちにとってとても力強いツールですが，もう１つ別の種類の辞書もあります。それは一言語だけを用いる辞書です。一言語だけを用いる辞書とは英英辞書のように１つの言語の辞書のことです。この種類の辞書は英語だけで書かれているので，英語の単語は翻訳されず，英語で説明されています。最初はそれらは難しく見えるかもしれませんが，英英辞書についてたくさんのよい点をお話しします。

　第１に，一言語だけを用いる辞書を使うと，新しい単語の使い方についてより注意深くなります。英和辞書を使うときには，私たちの多くは日本語の説明を見るだけです。それは速いですが，多くの場合，日本語の説明を見るだけでは英語を学ぶ助けにはなりません。一言語だけを用いる辞書を使えば，英語で書かれた説明と例文を何度も読まなければならないでしょう。全ての説明が英語なので，新しい単語の使い方をより明確に理解できます。さらに，一言語だけを用いる辞書は文の中での単語の使い方を示しているので，どの単語が，調べている新しい単語と一緒によく使われるかを示してくれます。

　第２に，一言語だけを用いる辞書を使えば，二言語を用いる辞書を使う場合よりももっと頻繁に単語を調

べるでしょう。あなたは説明の中の全ての単語を知っているわけではないかもしれないので，そこで再びその辞書を使います。たとえば，「発掘する」という単語を調べると，「古代のものを見つけるために注意深く掘る」という説明を目にするでしょう。もし，dig や ancient という単語を知らなければ，それらを調べなければならないでしょう。dig は「地面に穴をあける」と説明されています。ancient は「大昔から来ていること」を意味します。つまり，1 つの単語の代わりに，3 つの単語を学ぶことができるのです！　このようにして，説明の中に知らない単語を見つけると，その意味を理解するためにこれらの新しい単語を調べなくてはなりません。このことが英語を向上させる多くの機会を与えるのです。

　最後に，英英辞書は簡単な英語で単語を説明しているので，それらを使うことをおそれる必要はありません。英英辞書を作るとき，たいてい説明に使う単語を 2,000 語から 3,000 語選び（ふつう，選ばれた単語はとても簡単で，とても役に立つ単語です），その辞書の中ではそれらの単語だけを使います。また，辞書の最後の部分に選んだ単語のリストを見つけることができます。だから，そのリストを勉強し，何度もその辞書を使えば，いつの間にか最も重要な英語の単語を学んでいることでしょう！

　さあ，おそらく，もう英英辞書がどれだけ役に立ちうるかがはっきりとわかっているでしょう。最初は難しすぎるように見えるかもしれませんが，英語が本当に得意になりたいのなら，一言語だけを用いる辞書はとても役に立つでしょう。

4．(1)　恐竜について述べた第 1 段落を見る。「恐竜は絶滅してしまった種の例である」が第 1 段落の 4・5 文目の内容と合っている。

(2)　第 3 段落の 4 文目に「地球上に生息してきた全ての種の約 99.9 パーセントが今では絶滅してしまった」とあることから，「地球上に生息してきた動植物のほぼ 100 パーセントが現在では見られない」が適切。

(3)　人間による絶滅の主な原因が 5 つ挙げられている部分を見る。5 つ目に着目すると，「絶滅の原因の 1 つは，人間が木々を切り倒し，より多くのお金を得るために家屋を建てることである」とわかる。

(4)　北極グマ，パンダ，ゴリラ，トラ，そして多くの種類の植物について述べた最終段落を見る。「北極グマ，パンダ，ゴリラ，トラ，そして多くの種類の植物は，人間が環境を守ろうとしなければ，消えてしまうかもしれない」が適切。

(5)　ア．最後から 2 つ目の段落の 2 文目に着目する。固有の動物が自国の他の種を害しているのではなく，国家間の移動の発達により，他国の固有の種を害していると述べている。イ．「ほとんど全ての種類の動植物は，何百年以上もの間生き残ることができない」。第 3 段落の 4 文目や最終段落を見る。正しい。ウ．第 3 段落の最終文を見る。人間が現れてから，人間の活動によってほとんどの絶滅が起こされてきた。エ．「いくつかの種が本やテレビ番組のせいで絶滅するだろう」という記述はない。

【答】(1) ア　(2) ウ　(3) イ　(4) エ　(5) イ

◀全訳▶　大昔，地球上には恐竜が生息していました。彼らはのろのろした歩調で地面を歩き，水の中を泳ぎ，野原の上を飛びました。これは何百万年も前のことであり，このような時代が約 1 億 6,500 万年続きました。しかしある日，彼らは姿を消し，二度と戻ってきませんでした。恐竜は死に絶えましたが，いくつかの他の種は生き残りました。恐竜にとって環境の変化に適応することは困難でした。このような理由で，私たちは現在ここにいるのです。

　多くの様々な理由のために，いくつかの種にとって，その環境で生きることが困難となり，もはや次世代に引きつぐことができなくなります。つまり，これらの種のそれぞれは死に絶えてしまい，数年後には，私たちは地球上で彼らを全く見つけることができなくなるのです。これが，その種の「絶滅」です。動物や植物が絶滅の危機にあるとき，それらは「絶滅危惧種」と呼ばれます。

　絶滅には多くの理由があります。人間が現れる前，絶滅はしばしば起こっていました。変化していく環境の中で生き残ることができないと，その種は絶滅しました。科学者は，地球上に生息してきた全ての種の約 99.9 パーセントが今では絶滅してしまったと言います。人間が現れてから，特に，歴史が書き残されるよう

になってから，ほとんどの絶滅は人間の活動によって起きました。

人間による絶滅の主な原因は，

- ・乱獲：それらが必要なので，食用や科学，その他のそのような物事のためにある種が捕獲される。
- ・安全や事業のための殺害：ペット，農場の動物や作物を守るためにある種の全てが殺される。
- ・ペットとしての種の捕獲：ペットとして利用するためにある種が人間によって捕えられ，自然界から連れ去られる。
- ・汚染：産業廃棄物が原因で，種のすみかがもはや安全ではなくなり，その種が絶滅してしまう。
- ・森林破壊：森や野原が一掃され，家屋を販売することでお金を得るために利用され，そのため，種がすみかをなくし，絶滅してしまう。

これらの原因により，多くの種が危機に瀕しています。産業革命の前は，種の絶滅の主な原因は狩猟を通して殺しすぎることでした。しかし，産業革命のあとは，種のすみかを破壊することが主な原因となっています。広大な土地を失うことだけでなく種のすみかに対する小さな変化でさえも，絶滅を引き起こす可能性があります。これは，そのことが，種が動き回り，お互いにコミュニケーションをとることを妨げるからです。繁殖することができなくなるので，これは種にとって大きな問題となります。たとえば，ほんの数本の道路を造ることが，中国のパンダがお互いに出会うことを妨げる可能性があると科学者は言います。パンダは道路を横断しないからです。パンダが移動するために橋が建設されると，パンダの数が再び少し増加しました。

国家間のコミュニケーションを通じて私たちの世界がより小さくなるにつれて，そのこともまた絶滅を引き起こしています。国家間の移動の発達は，多くの動物が人間とともに世界中を移動し，その結果，多くの国々の固有の種を害するということを意味しています。世界中の人々は，遠くの場所に存在する動植物を所有して楽しみます。それは，多くの動物が危機に瀕しているということを意味します。毎年，多くの動植物が，発展途上国から，豊かな先進国へと持ち込まれています。国家間のこのようなやりとりによって，人々の楽しみのためだけに，多くの動物が捕えられ，外国へ送られています。

今日，北極グマ，パンダ，ゴリラ，トラ，そして多くの種類の植物は全て私たちによく知られていますが，もしすぐにでも何かしなければ，私たちの子どもたちがそれらを見る唯一の方法は，本や昔のテレビ番組の中になってしまうでしょう。

5. (1) ポールの面倒をよく見てくれた兄のトムが，父親の仕事を手伝い始めたと述べている場面。「トムも忙しくなり，ポールとあまり時間を過ごせなくなった（ⅰ）」→「しかし，彼はポールのことをとても愛していたので，常に彼のことを気にかけていた（ⅲ）」→「毎年，ポールの誕生日に，彼はすばらしい贈り物をあげた（ⅱ）」という流れ。

(2) ポールはクリスマスプレゼント「として」トムから車を受けとった。「～として」＝ as ～。

(3) 第6段落で，ポールは少年が「彼のようなお兄さんが欲しい」と言うと思っていたけれど，少年は「彼のようなお兄さんになりたい」と言っており，ポールの予想とは違っていたことに着目する。ポールは，少年が家まで大きな車に乗ることができたのを近所の人に見せたいのだろうと思っていたが，その予想は「間違って」いたと考えられる。

(4) 第3段落を見る。ポールに贈り物をよくあげていた兄のトムは，「どんな贈り物をもらうよりも，お前の笑顔が僕を幸せにしてくれるんだ」といつも言っていたことに着目する。少年の兄弟の様子を見て，ポールは「受けとることより与えることの方が幸せだ」ということを学んだ。

(5) ア．「ポールの母親が亡くなったとき，彼の父親はレストランを10軒以上経営していた」とは述べられていない。イ．第4段落の1・2文目を見る。ポールはクリスマスプレゼントとして車をもらった数日後に自動車運転免許証を取得した。ウ．第6段落を見る。少年はトムのような兄が欲しいと言ったのではなく，トムのようになりたいと言った。エ．「ポールは少年と少年の弟と一緒にドライブに出かけた」。第11段落

の１・２文目を見る。正しい。

【答】(1) イ　(2) ウ　(3) エ　(4) ウ　(5) エ

◀全訳▶　ポールは裕福な家庭に生まれました。彼の家族はニューヨークで暮らしていて，父親は５軒のレストランを経営していました。ポールが２歳のときに，母親が亡くなりました。そのため，彼には母親の思い出が何もありませんでした。父親は一度も再婚しませんでした。

　ポールにはトムという兄がいました。彼はポールよりも10歳年上でした。ポールが５歳のときに，父親はさらに５軒のレストランを開店させました。彼はとても忙しくなりました。彼は毎日家に帰り，彼らと一緒に多くの時間を過ごしたいと思いましたが，できませんでした。そのため，トムがとてもよくポールの面倒を見ました。

　ポールが12歳のときに，トムは父親の仕事を手伝い始めました。トムも忙しくなり，ポールとあまり時間を過ごせなくなりました。しかし，彼はポールのことをとても愛していたので，常に彼のことを気にかけていました。毎年，ポールの誕生日に，彼はすばらしい贈り物をあげました。そして，クリスマスイブの日には，彼はポールの欲しいものは何でも買ってあげました。しかし，ポールには十分なお金がなかったので，トムに何も贈り物を買いませんでした。ポールが笑顔で「ありがとう。とても気に入ったよ。お兄ちゃんに何もあげられなくてごめん」と言うと，トムはいつも「いいんだ。どんな贈り物をもらうよりも，お前の笑顔が僕を幸せにしてくれるんだ」と言いました。

　18歳のとき，ポールはクリスマスプレゼントとしてトムから車を受けとりました。数日後のクリスマスイブ直前に，彼は自動車運転免許証を取得しました。クリスマスイブの日にドライブをしようとポールが家を出ると，１人の少年がその新しい車の周りを歩いていて，「これはあなたの車ですか？」とたずねました。

　「そうだよ。兄がクリスマスに僕にくれたんだ」とポールは答えました。少年は驚いて「お兄さんがあなたにそれをくれて，あなたは全くお金を払わなかったということですか？　へえ，僕は…」と言いました。

　もちろん，ポールには少年が言おうとしていることがわかりました。ポールは彼が「へえ，僕は彼のようなお兄さんが欲しいな」と言うだろうと思ったのです。しかし，ポールは少年の言葉に驚きました。彼は「僕はあなたのお兄さんのようになりたいな」と言ったのです。

　ポールは彼のことを知りませんでしたが，いい子だなと思いました。ポールは彼のことが気に入ったので，「僕の車に乗ってみない？」とたずねました。「はい，はい！」と少年は答えました。彼らは車に乗り，ドライブに出かけました。

　しばらくすると，少年は「この車で僕の家まで連れていってくれませんか？」と言いました。ポールは笑顔で「もちろん」と言いました。ポールは，少年が家まで大きな車に乗ることができたのを近所の人に見せたいのだろうと思いました。しかし，ポールは再び間違えました。「２つ階段がある家の前で車をとめてくれませんか？」と少年は頼みました。

　車から出ると，彼は階段を走ってのぼり，家の中に入っていきました。そして，間もなく，ゆっくりと戻ってきました。彼は弟を抱いていました。彼は自分で歩くことができなかったのです。彼らは一緒に一番下の階段に座りました。少年は車を指さしました。

　「あれが家の中でお前に話した車だよ。彼のお兄さんがクリスマスにくれて，彼は全くお金を払わなかったんだ。いつか僕もあんな車をお前にあげるよ。そうすれば，何度も何度も話したクリスマスの素敵なものを全部お前は自分で見ることができる」　この言葉を聞いて，ポールはもう少しで泣くところでした。

　ポールは車から降りて，少年の弟を車の前の座席まで運びました。少年は弟の隣に座り，彼ら３人はドライブに出かけました。ポールは彼らを街の中心部まで連れていき，店のきれいなショーウィンドーを見せました。少年の弟は車に乗り，生まれて初めてそこへ行きました。見るもの全てが彼にとって初めてのものでした。彼はとてもわくわくしていました。少年が彼にほほえみました。それはポールをとても幸せな気持ちにしました。それはすばらしい時間でした。

「受けとることよりも与えることの方が幸せなんだ」 トムはいつもポールに言っていました。そのクリスマスイブの日に，ポールはその理由を理解しました。

Chapter3 *Writing* 解答・解説

（48 ページ）

1. 「学校で昼食をとる場合，あなたは弁当と給食のどちらがいいですか？ あなたの意見と理由を 50 語程度の英語で書きなさい」。

【答】bento ／ I like bentos better. The school lunch is too much for me and sometimes has food I can't eat for health reasons. Bentos have food I can eat and are less expensive because usually the food left from dinner the night before is put in bentos.（46 語）

school lunch ／ I think the school lunch is better. It is difficult for my mother to make lunch for me every day and I have no time to make lunch for myself before going to school. If we buy a bento at a store, maybe it is not healthy, but the school lunch is healthy.（53 語）

2. 「環境を保護するためにあなたが何をしているか述べなさい。50 語程度の英語で書きなさい」。

【答】There are some things I always do for the environment. For example, I use less electricity. My parents often leave the lights on, but I turn them off. And I also try not to waste food. I don't buy any food I don't need, and I eat up the food which is served to me.（55 語）

3. 「あなたはどの国に興味がありますか？ なぜその国に興味があるか述べなさい。50 語程度の英語で書きなさい」。

【答】I'm interested in Italy, because I like Leonardo da Vinci. He not only created many drawings and paintings but also designed some machines. I have learned about him by reading books and seeing his works at museums. I want to see his country with my own eyes.（47 語）

4. 「生徒が携帯電話を校内へ持ち込むことを許可している学校があります。あなたは携帯電話の校内への持ち込みに賛成ですか？ それとも反対ですか？ 賛成ならば Yes，反対ならば No と書き，理由を 50 語程度の英語で書きなさい」。

【答】賛成の場合／ Yes. We can carry our cell phones, if we don't use them during lessons. And cell phones are necessary in our daily lives. For example, when our family members need to call us about something important immediately, cell phones are useful. So I think we should be able to carry our cell phones in school.（55 語）

反対の場合／ No. We don't need to carry our cell phones in school. If we use our cell phones to talk, write e-mails, or play games during breaks, we won't be able to pay enough attention to classwork during lessons because we may keep thinking about what we were doing during the break.（51 語）

5. 「現在，日本には 24 時間営業のコンビニエンスストアがたくさんあります。あなたはそれが私たちにとってよいと思いますか？ それとも悪いと思いますか？ あなたの意見を 50 語程度の英語で書きなさい」。

【答】よいと思う場合／ There are many convenience stores and I think it is very good for us. Today many people are working in the early morning or at night. They sometimes want to buy something to drink or eat at night. Then they can go to a 24-hour convenience store and buy something.（50 語）

悪いと思う場合／ There are many convenience stores in Japan, but are they really necessary? Japan imports most of the energy resources, so we must save energy. But convenience stores are open at night and use a lot of electricity. If convenience stores are closed at night, we can save a lot of energy.（51 語）

6．「カナダからの留学生があなたの学校を 2 週間訪問します。あなたはその留学生に日本の国民の祝日について話します。『こどもの日』と『敬老の日』のどちらの祝日を選びますか？　そして，それはなぜですか？　『こどもの日』と『敬老の日』のどちらかを○で囲み，理由を与えられた英語に続けて 50 語程度の英語で書きなさい。与えられた英語は語数に含みません」。

　【答】こどもの日／(I would like to choose Children's Day, because) I think it will be interesting for the student to know about koinobori seen in Japan on that day. Koinobori is a large carp-shaped streamer made of paper or cloth. I'll tell the student that we hope children will have a good future and grow up healthy by putting them up in the sky.（54 語）

　敬老の日／(I would like to choose Respect for the Aged Day, because) it is very important for us to be kind to old people both in Japan and Canada. Some people don't care about old people, and other people do. We should think more about old people, and I want to help them when they need help.（45 語）

7．「自己紹介をして，あなたにとって大切なものについて述べなさい。なぜそれが大切なのか述べなさい。50 語程度の英語で書きなさい」。

　【答】Hello, my name is Mika. The violin which my father gave me is important to me. I started taking violin lessons when I was ten, and he gave it to me then. The violin is about fifty years old. Sometimes it sounds very beautiful and sometimes it doesn't. I enjoy playing it every day.（54 語）

8．「国際的な人間になるためには，私たちは英語以外に何を学ぶべきですか？　50 語程度の英語で書きなさい」。

　【答】Traveling overseas, studying the histories and cultures of various countries, and making friends from around the world encourage global thinking. These activities help us learn a lot about foreign people's ways of thinking. By doing so, people can understand each other better, and understanding each other makes the world a better place.（52 語）

Chapter4 *Listening* 解答・解説

（52 ページ）

【 Part A 】

No.1. 1．アは「男性にコンピュータの起動方法を教える」という意味。イは「男性に手助けをしてくれる人を呼ぶように言う」という意味。ウは「男性を手助けしてくれる人を呼ぶ」という意味。エは「男性のためにコンピュータを起動する」という意味。

　　2．アは「女性は毎晩早く寝るべきだ」という意味。イは「女性は寝るのをやめるべきだ」という意味。ウは「女性は何かをしたいと思うべきだ」という意味。エは「女性は家に帰って寝るべきだ」という意味。not 〜 anything は「何も〜ない」という意味。

　　3．アは「彼はポケットの中に自分の携帯電話を見つけた」という意味。イは「彼は女性の携帯電話をなくした」という意味。ウは「彼は電車で携帯電話をなくした」という意味。エは「彼は自分の携帯電話を見つけるように女性に頼んだ」という意味。

　　4．女性は花とクッキーを持っていく。花については，桜が手に入らないので，バラを持っていく。

　　5．アは「うれしくてわくわくしている」という意味。イは「悲しくて疲れている」という意味。ウは「赤ちゃんがかわいそうだと思っている」という意味。エは「その知らせに驚いている」という意味。

6．アは「女性を一緒に長野に連れていく」という意味。イは「女性をおじに紹介する」という意味。ウは「長野で野菜を育てる」という意味。エは「女性に野菜を送る」という意味。

【答】1．ウ　2．エ　3．ア　4．ウ　5．ア　6．エ

◀全訳▶

1．男性：このコンピュータを使いたいのですが。どうやって起動させるのか教えてくれませんか？

　　女性：すみません，私にもわかりません。だれか手助けしてくれる人を呼びます。

　　質問：女性がおそらくすることは何ですか？

2．女性：すごく眠いから，何もしたくないわ。

　　男性：もう家に帰って寝たほうがいいよ。

　　質問：男性が意味していることは何ですか？

3．男性：どうしよう！　携帯電話をどこかでなくした。

　　女性：何ですって？　電車の中に忘れたんじゃないの？　そこで使っていたわよ。

　　男性：ああ，思い出した。ポケットに入れたんだ。ほら，あったよ。

　　質問：男性は何をしましたか？

4．女性：今度の土曜日にパーティーへ行くの。

　　男性：何のパーティー？

　　女性：中国出身の友達が誕生日パーティーに招待してくれたの。

　　男性：そのパーティーに何か持っていくの？

　　女性：うん。彼女の好きな花を持っていくつもりよ。それから，クッキーを作って彼女にあげるわ。

　　男性：彼女は何の花が好きなの？

　　女性：桜が好きだけれど，今は手に入らないからバラを持っていくわ。彼女はバラも好きなのよ。

　　男性：それはいいね。楽しんできてね。

　　女性：ありがとう。

　　質問：女性は友達のパーティーに何を持っていくでしょうか？

5．男の子：やあ，スーザン。すごくうれしそうだね。

　　女の子：姉が先週赤ちゃんを産んだの。この写真を見て。

　　男の子：この子は男の子なの，それとも女の子？

　　女の子：男の子よ。本当にかわいいと思わない？

　　男の子：本当だね。とても小さくてかわいいね。もう彼と会ったの？

　　女の子：まだよ。明日会うの。すごく楽しみにしているの。

　　質問：女の子はどのような気持ちですか？

6．男性：来週，長野のおじを訪ねるんだ。

　　女性：なんてすてきなの！　おじさんは何の仕事をしているの？

　　男性：いろいろな種類の野菜をたくさん育てているよ。トマト，レタス，トウモロコシや他にもたくさん。僕たちはそれらを毎日食べるんだよ。

　　女性：きっとそれらはとてもおいしいわね。

　　男性：そうなんだ。もしよかったら，君に送ってあげるよ。

　　女性：ありがとう。

　　質問：男性がおそらくすることは何ですか？

No.2. 1．女性は He said he had a plane to catch. と言っている。

　　2．miss ～＝「～がいなくて寂しい，～が恋しい」。

　　3．アは「女性と一緒に病院へ行く」という意味。イは「女性を病院に連れていく」という意味。ウは「女

性の猫を駅へ連れていく」という意味。エは「女性の猫を病院に連れていく」という意味。

4．男性は魚が好きではない。好きなものは，フライドチキンと米とトマト。

5．女の子は It's almost six in the evening.と言っているので，「午後 6 時の少し前」が適切。

6．アは「彼女の母親に待つように頼むこと」という意味。イは「彼女の携帯電話をとりに家に帰ること」という意味。ウは「彼女の先生に電話をするために男性の携帯電話を借りること」という意味。エは「彼女の先生に会いに駅へ行くこと」という意味。

【答】1．エ　2．ア　3．エ　4．ウ　5．ア　6．ウ

◀全訳▶

1．男性：ケンがさっきすごい速さで走っていたよ。
　　女性：乗らなければならない飛行機があると言っていたわ。
　　質問：ケンはどこに向かっていましたか？

2．女性：明日，インドに出発するわ。2 週間後に戻るわね。
　　男性：君がいないと寂しいよ。
　　質問：男性はどのような気持ちですか？

3．男性：悲しそうだね。どうしたの？
　　女性：私の猫が病気なの。昨日から彼女は何も食べていないの。私のかわりに病院に連れていってくれない？
　　男性：いいよ。
　　質問：男性がおそらくすることは何ですか？

4．女性：今度の日曜日に夕食を食べに私の家に来ない？
　　男性：行きたいけれど，僕たちは何を食べることになるのかな？
　　女性：どういうこと？
　　男性：申し訳ないけれど，僕は魚が好きではないんだよ。
　　女性：あら，それは知らなかった。では，何が好きなの？
　　男性：フライドチキンが大好きなんだ。そして，米とトマトも好きだよ。
　　女性：わかったわ。でも，なぜ魚が好きではないの？
　　男性：12 歳のとき，悪くなった魚を食べたんだ。それで，すごく具合が悪くなってね。2, 3 日の間寝込んだよ。
　　女性：なるほどね。
　　質問：女性が次の日曜日の夕食におそらく出すものは何ですか？

5．男の子：もしもし。ニューヨークはどんな天気だい？
　　女の子：とても寒いわ。今朝は気温が本当に低かったわ。でも，正午までに上がってまた下がったの。
　　男の子：今，何時？
　　女の子：もうすぐ午後 6 時よ。
　　男の子：外はもう暗い？
　　女の子：ええ。少し前に日が沈んだわ。
　　質問：ニューヨークは何時ですか？

6．男性：やあ，アン，どうしたの？
　　女性：困っていることがあるの。母を迎えに駅まで行かなければならないんだけれど，学校で先生にも会わなければならないの。
　　男性：お母さんに電話して，待ってくれるように頼んだらどう？
　　女性：そうしたいけれど，携帯電話を家に忘れたの。

男性：それはまずいね。先生ってだれだい？　ジョンソン先生なら，電話番号を知っているよ。

女性：あなたの携帯電話を使ってもいい？　今から先生に電話するわ。

質問：女性の考えは何ですか？

【 Part B 】

No.1. (1)　夜遅くまで勉強した理由として I had a lot of math homework と言っている。

(2)　マサコは It is difficult to understand how others feel, but it is important to try. と言っている。

【答】(1) エ　(2) ア

◆全訳▶　みなさん，こんにちは。今日は，祖父のことについてお話しします。私は祖父のことが大好きです。

彼は 75 歳ですが，とても若く見えます。彼は私にとてもやさしくしてくれます。彼は他の人々や動物に対してもやさしくします。例えば，私たちはシロという名前の犬を飼っています。シロは公園の周りを歩くことが好きです。もちろん，シロは話すことができませんが，祖父はシロのことを理解しています。毎朝そして毎晩，祖父はシロと一緒に公園の周りを歩きます。シロは祖父と一緒にいて，とてもうれしそうです。

先週，数学の宿題がたくさんあったので，私は夜遅くまでとても一生懸命数学の勉強をしました。祖父が部屋に入ってきて「ホットミルクを飲みなさい，マサコ」と言いました。私は何か飲み物がほしいと思っていたので，驚きました。どのようにして彼はそのことがわかったのでしょう？　彼はただほほえんで，家族だから私のことがわかるのだと言いました。

私は今では祖父の言葉が理解できます。他人がどのように感じているかを理解するのは困難ですが，しようとすることが大切なのです。私は将来，祖父のようにやさしくなりたいと思います。

質問１：マサコはなぜ夜遅くまで数学の勉強をしましたか？

質問２：マサコは祖父から何を学びましたか？

No.2. (1)　タクヤがとても喜んだ理由は，サッカーボールをもらったから。

(2)　祭りを通して，人々は地球を救うために何をすればよいか学ぶことができる。

【答】(1) イ　(2) ウ

◆全訳▶　あなたたちは地球によいことを何かしていますか？　今日私は，私たちの町がしていることについて話したいと思います。

毎年，11 月の最初の日曜日に，私たちの町では，ナカマチフェスティバルと呼ばれる祭りがチュウオウ公園であります。あなたたちはその祭りに行ったことがありますか？　その祭りで，人々は地球のために何をすることができるかということについて，考えることができます。

その祭りは私の家の近くであるので，私は普通，母と弟のタクヤと一緒にそこへ行きます。その祭りにはいくつかの人気のある見るべきものがあります。１つはミュージックコンサートです。人々は音楽を楽しみ，地球を救うことについての歌を歌います。もう１つは，ふれあいマーケットです。たくさんの家族やグループが，使わなくなったものを持って来て，そこで売ります。ほかの人たちは，それらのものを買って楽しみます。あなたたちは，まだ使うことができるよいものをたくさん見つけることができます。コンサートもマーケットも両方とも人気があり，地球のためによいものです。

去年，私はふれあいマーケットでテニスラケットを買いました。そのあと，私はよいサッカーボールを見つけました。タクヤは学校でサッカーの試合があったので，私たちと一緒に来ることができませんでした。私は，彼が自分のボールをほしいと思っていることを知っていました。だから，私は母と話して，彼にそのボールを買いました。彼が帰って来たとき，私は彼にそれを渡しました。彼はとても喜びました。

今年は祭りを見に来てください。この祭りを通して，大切な何かを学ぶことができます。それは私たちに，地球を救うために何をすべきか教えてくれます。

質問１：タクヤはなぜとても喜んだのですか？

質問２：その祭りを通して，人々は何を学ぶことができますか？

【 Part C 】

No.1. 会話の内容をおおまかにまとめると，①「動物をおりの中で飼う動物園について」→②「自然に近い環境で動物を飼う動物園について」→③「動物園の動物の寿命が野生動物より長いということについて」。リサは，①については，その種類の動物園は，人間にとってはよいが動物にとってはよくないと思っている。理由は，動物に自由がないから。②については，その種類の動物園は人間にも動物にもよいと思っている。理由は，人間はよい経験ができ，自然に近い環境にいる動物のほうが幸せだから。③については，動物園の動物が野生動物より長生きなのはよいことだが，それが幸せかどうかはわからないと思っている。理由は，人間には動物がどう思っているかわからないから。

【答】Lisa thinks a zoo which keeps animals in cages is good for people but not a good living place for animals because people enjoy seeing animals but the animals are not free and are not happy.

She thinks a zoo with a near-natural environment is good for people and animals because it can give visitors good experiences and the animals in a near-natural environment are happier.

Lisa thinks that even though animals kept in a zoo live longer than wild animals, those in a zoo may not be happy because there's no way to know how they feel.

◀全訳▶ 動物園の発達

おそらく，あなたたちのほとんどは動物園を訪れたことがあるでしょう。動物園がどのように発達してきたか知っていますか？

1828年，最初の近代的な動物園のロンドン動物園が，ロンドンに開園しました。その動物園は，研究のために多くのいろいろな種類の動物を見せていました。ロンドンに続いて，アムステルダムやベルリンといった他の多くの大都市が自身の動物園を持ち始めました。

最初は，動物はおりの中で飼育されていました。しかし，1980年代から，アメリカの動物園は動物を人に見せる方法を変えてきました。そのような動物園では，動物は自然に近い環境で暮らしています。動物の周りの草や木や岩は，本物であるか，とても本物らしく見えます。おそらく，そのような動物はこういった環境にいるほうがずっと幸せでしょう。

現在では，動物により近づく機会を提供することができる動物園がたくさんあります。動物を見るだけでなく，触ったりえさをあげたりすることもできます。そのような動物園の一つを訪れて，動物について勉強してみたらどうですか？

ジャック：リサ，動物園の発達に関する文章は気に入った？

リサ　　：そうね，最初は動物園にあまり興味はなかったけれど，この文章を読んだら，動物園にすごく行きたくなったわ。

ジャック：動物をおりの中で飼育している動物園をどう思う？

リサ　　：私が小さいころは，そういう種類の動物園しか知らなかったわ。両親は家の近くの動物園にときどき連れていってくれて，楽しんだわ。動物園を訪れる人は動物を見て楽しむから，動物園は人間にとっていいものだわ。でも，今は動物園は動物にとっていい場所ではないと思う。自分がおりの中で飼育されていると想像してみて。住む場所と十分な食べものはある。でも，一生そのおりから出られない。そんな状況で暮らしたくないわ。

ジャック：君の言うことはわかるよ。でも，もし一生その状況なら，君はそれが快適だと思うだろう。もし周囲のみんながそのように暮らしているなら，だれもそれがおかしいとは思わない。

リサ　　：そのとおりかもしれない。でも，それでもおりの中の動物は幸せではないと思う。

ジャック：ええと，それなら，自然に近い環境にいる動物を見たいの？

リサ　　：もちろんそういう動物のほうが興味深いけれど，それらは野生動物ではないわ。

ジャック：どういうこと？

リサ　　：動物の周りの環境は自然に近いけれど，本物の自然ほどよくないわ。

ジャック：なるほど。そういう動物園はよくないと思うの？

リサ　　：動物にとってはとてもよいと思うわ。そういう動物園の動物はおりの中の動物より幸せよ。でも，それでもそれらは食べものを与えられている。ということは，野生の環境で暮らしていないということよ。野生動物は自分で食べものを探して手に入れなければならない。もしできなければ，死んでしまう。動物園の動物は違うわ。

ジャック：わかった。僕は，そういう動物園は小さな子供にとってはいいと思う。親が子供をそういう動物園に連れていって，子供は動物を見たり，触ったり，食べものをあげたり，そして，一緒に写真を撮ることだってできる。その体験は子供にとても楽しい思い出を与えてくれるし，彼らは大人になってもずっと動物に興味をもっているかもしれない。

リサ　　：同感だわ。

ジャック：ところで，人間に世話をされている動物は野生動物よりも長生きだと知っている？

リサ　　：どのくらい長生きなの？

ジャック：例えば，ある研究によると，ある種の猿は野生の環境では25年から30年までしか生きないけれど，動物園で飼育されると35年ほど生きるんだ。ほとんどすべての動物は，野生の環境にいるよりも動物園にいるほうが長生きするし，動物園の動物の中には，ずっと長生きする動物もいるんだよ。

リサ　　：それはおもしろいわね。長生きはいいことだけれど，必ずしもそれが幸せであることを意味するとは限らないわ。

ジャック：同じことが人間についても言えるかもしれない。人間は長生きがいいことだと言うけれど，高齢者の中には，家族や友人がもう亡くなっているから寂しいとよく言っている人もいるよ。

リサ　　：動物にとって，それは難しい問題ね。動物がどう感じているか私たちにはわからないから。

質問：リサは動物園についてどう思っていますか？　彼女の意見と理由を英語で説明しなさい。書く時間は5分です。始めなさい。

No.2. 会話の主な内容をまとめると，次のとおり。ケビンの意見は，「スマートフォンはすごく役に立つ。スマートフォンで本や辞書が見られるので，勉強の役に立つ」。ヘレンの意見は，「使いすぎると目や睡眠に悪影響がある。歩きながらスマートフォンを使うと危険だ。スマートフォンの中に重要な情報が入っているので，なくすと大変なことになる」。「スマートフォンの光による健康被害」，「歩きながらのスマートフォン使用の危険性」，「大切な情報が入っていることによる紛失の重大性」についてまとめるとよい。

【答】Helen thinks that there are some bad points about smartphones.

　She thinks they are sometimes bad for our health because the light from smartphones can be not good for our eyes and sleep.

　She also thinks smartphones can be dangerous because many people use them when they walk on a street or on the platform of a station.

　Helen thinks that if smartphones are lost, that will be a serious problem, because the information on them is very important.

◀全訳▶　　　　　　　　　　スマートフォンはどのくらい役に立つか？

　あなたはスマートフォンを持っていますか？　たぶん持っているでしょう。若者はそれらなしでは生きていけないとよく言います。確かに，スマートフォンはとても役に立ちます。なぜなら，もし持っていれば，地図を見たり，本や雑誌を読んだり，電車の時刻表を見つけたり，写真やビデオを撮ったり，それらを友達と共有したりするような多くのことができるからです。本や雑誌をスマートフォンで読むことは，紙の本や雑誌を読むことよりもお金がかかりません。そしてまた，これらのデジタル・コンテンツのほうが，紙の無駄

づかいがかなり減るので環境にもいいのです。

　一方で，スマートフォンを使うことには悪い点がいくつかあります。学生は，スマートフォンで話したり，メールを送ったり，ゲームをすることに忙しすぎて，勉強をする時間がほとんどありません。スマートフォンにあまりにも多くの時間を費やすことは，目を傷つけたり睡眠に影響を与えたりする場合もあります。

　スマートフォンは，将来ますます便利になるでしょう。そして，それらなしでは生きていけない人がますます増えるでしょう。

ケビン：ヘレン，スマートフォンに関する文章を読んだ？

ヘレン：ええ，読んだわ。ケビン，あなたはスマートフォンについてどう思う？

ケビン：実は，2，3か月前にスマートフォンを買って，すごく役に立つとわかったんだ。電車の中で，スマートフォンではなくて携帯電話を使っている人を見ると，なぜスマートフォンを持たないのかと思う。スマートフォンのほうがずっといいから，スマートフォンを買うように彼らに言いたいよ。

ヘレン：なるほど。私自身も１台持っているけれど，スマートフォンは他の電話より高額よね。それに，スマートフォンについては悪い点がたくさんあると思う。例えば，その文章にも書いてあるように，スマートフォンから来る光を長時間見ることは，目を傷つける場合があるわ。そして，寝る直前にその光を見ると，よく眠れなくなるかもしれない。

ケビン：そのとおり。スマートフォンに費やす時間を減らすようにしているよ，特に夜はね。でも，よくしでかすけれど。

ヘレン：わかるわ。それを使っているときは，時間がたつのが本当にはやいわ。それから，スマートフォンについて言いたいことが別にあるの。

ケビン：何だい？

ヘレン：路上や駅のホームを歩いているときにスマートフォンを使っている人が大勢いるわ。とても危険よ。路上でスマートフォンを見ている女の人をかつて見たわ。信号が赤なのに道を渡っていたの！　幸い，自動車にはひかれなかったけれどね。

ケビン：僕もそういう人を見るよ。それは悪い点だね。スマートフォンが僕たちから勉強する時間をたくさん奪うことは本当だけれど，スマートフォンを勉強のために使うことができるよ。

ヘレン：どういう意味？

ケビン：スマートフォンには本や雑誌だけでなくたくさんの辞書も搭載されているから，宿題をしたりレポートを書いたりするときにはそういう辞書を使うよ。紙の辞書よりも持ち運ぶのに軽いし。両親は，学生時代にとても重い本や辞書を持ち運ばなければならなかったと言っているよ。

ヘレン：あら，私の両親は同じことを言っているわ。もう一つのとても悪い点は，スマートフォンをなくしたら，とても重大な問題になるということね。あなたは友達や家族の電話番号を覚えている？

ケビン：いいや。長すぎて覚えられないよ。それらはすべてスマートフォンの中に登録されているよ。

ヘレン：スマートフォンを持っているほとんどの人は同じ状況にいるわ。電話番号，メールアドレス，メールのメッセージ，写真，その他の大切な情報が全部スマートフォンの中にあるの。絶対にスマートフォンをなくしてはいけないわね。

ケビン：同感だね。

ヘレン：スマートフォンについて悪い点をいくつか言ったけれど，私はきっと，将来，自分のスマートフォンを使い続けるわ。

ケビン：僕もだよ。

質問：ヘレンはスマートフォンについてどう思っていますか？　彼女の意見と理由を英語で説明しなさい。書く時間は５分です。始めなさい。

─────〈スクリプト〉─────

【 Part A 】

No.1

1	Man：	I want to use this computer. Can you tell me how to start it?
	Woman：	I'm sorry, I don't know, either. I'll call someone to help you.
	Question：	What will the woman probably do?
2	Woman：	I'm very sleepy, so I don't want to do anything.
	Man：	You should go home now and get some sleep.
	Question：	What does the man mean?
3	Man：	Oh my god! I've lost my cell phone somewhere.
	Woman：	What? Didn't you leave it on the train? You were using it there.
	Man：	Now I remember. I put it in my pocket. Here it is.
	Question：	What did the man do?
4	Woman：	I'm going to a party next Saturday.
	Man：	What party is it?
	Woman：	My friend from China has invited me to her birthday party.
	Man：	Are you going to take something to the party?
	Woman：	Yes. I'm going to take some flowers she likes. And I'm going to make some cookies and give them to her.
	Man：	What flowers does she like?
	Woman：	She likes cherry blossoms, but I can't get those flowers now, so I'll take some roses. She likes roses, too.
	Man：	Sounds nice. Have a good time.
	Woman：	Thank you.
	Question：	What will the woman take to her friend's party?
5	Boy：	Hi, Susan. You look very happy.
	Girl：	My sister had a baby last week. Look at this photo.
	Boy：	Is this a boy or a girl?
	Girl：	A boy. He's really cute, don't you think?
	Boy：	He really is. He is very small and cute. Have you seen him yet?
	Girl：	No. I'm going to see him tomorrow. I'm really looking forward to it.
	Question：	How does the girl feel?
6	Man：	I'm going to visit my uncle in Nagano next week.
	Woman：	How wonderful! What does he do?
	Man：	He grows many different kinds of vegetables. Tomatoes, lettuce, corn, and many other things. We eat them every day.
	Woman：	I'm sure they taste very good.
	Man：	Yes. I'll send you some if you want.
	Woman：	Thanks.
	Question：	What will the man probably do?

No.2

1   Man ： Ken was running so fast a few minutes ago.

    Woman ： He said he had a plane to catch.

   Question ： Where was Ken going?

2   Woman ： I'm leaving for India tomorrow. I'll be back in two weeks.

      Man ： I will miss you.

   Question ： How does the man feel?

3   Man ： You look sad. What happened?

    Woman ： My cat is sick. She hasn't eaten anything since yesterday. Can you take her to the hospital for me?

      Man ： Sure.

   Question ： What will the man probably do?

4   Woman ： Can you come to my house for dinner next Sunday?

      Man ： I want to come, but what are we going to eat?

    Woman ： What do you mean?

      Man ： I'm sorry but I don't like fish.

    Woman ： Oh, I didn't know that. What do you like, then?

      Man ： I like fried chicken very much. And I like rice and tomatoes, too.

    Woman ： OK. But why don't you like fish?

      Man ： When I was twelve, I ate fish which was bad. It made me very sick. I had to stay in bed for a few days.

    Woman ： I see.

   Question ： What will the woman probably serve for dinner next Sunday?

5   Boy ： Hello. How's the weather there in New York?

     Girl ： Very cold. The temperature was really low this morning. But it went up by noon and went down again.

     Boy ： What time is it?

     Girl ： It's almost six in the evening.

     Boy ： Is it already dark outside?

     Girl ： Yes. The sun went down a while ago.

   Question ： What time is it in New York?

6   Man ： Hi, Ann, what's up?

    Woman ： I have a problem. I have to go to the station to meet my mother, but I have to see my teacher at school, too.

      Man ： Why don't you call and ask your mother to wait?

    Woman ： I want to do so, but I left my cell phone at home.

      Man ： That's bad. Who's your teacher? If that's Mr. Johnson, I know his number.

    Woman ： Can I use your cell phone? I'll call him now.

   Question ： What is the woman's idea?

───────────〈スクリプト〉───────────

【 Part B 】

No.1

Hello, everyone. Today I am going to talk about my grandfather. I love him very much.

He is seventy-five years old, but he looks very young. He is very kind to me. He is also kind to other people and animals. For example, we have a dog named Shiro. Shiro likes to walk around the park. Of course, Shiro cannot speak, but my grandfather understands Shiro. Every morning and evening, my grandfather walks around the park with Shiro. Shiro looks very happy to be with him.

Last week, I studied math very hard until late at night because I had a lot of math homework. My grandfather came into my room and said, "Have some hot milk, Masako." I was surprised because I wanted something to drink. How did he know? He just smiled and said that he understands me because we are family.

Now I understand my grandfather's words. It is difficult to understand how others feel, but it is important to try. I want to be kind like my grandfather in the future.

Question 1： Why did Masako study math until late at night?

Question 2： What did Masako learn from her grandfather?

No.2

Are you doing anything good for the earth? Today I will tell you about something our city does.

Every year on the first Sunday of November, our city has a festival called the Nakamachi Festival at Chuo Park. Have you ever been to the festival? At the festival people can think about what they can do for the earth.

The festival is near my house and I usually go there with my mother and my brother Takuya. There are some popular things to see at the festival. One is a music concert. People enjoy music and sing songs about saving the earth. Another is the Fureai Market. A lot of families and groups bring things they don't use and sell them there. Other people enjoy buying those things. You can find many good things you can still use. Both the concert and the market are popular and good for the earth.

Last year I bought a tennis racket at the Fureai Market. Then I found a nice soccer ball. Takuya couldn't come with us because he had a soccer game at his school. I knew he wanted his own ball. So I talked with my mother and bought the ball for him. I gave it to him when he came home. He was very happy.

Come and see the festival this year. You can learn something important through this festival. It teaches us what to do to help the earth.

Question 1： Why was Takuya very happy?

Question 2： What can people learn through the festival?

―〈スクリプト〉―

【 Part C 】

No.1

Jack ： Lisa, did you like the passage about the development of zoos?

Lisa ： Well, at first I wasn't very interested in zoos, but after reading this passage, I really want to go to a zoo.

Jack ： What do you think about zoos that keep animals in cages?

Lisa ： When I was a little girl, I knew only that kind of zoos. My parents sometimes took me to the zoo near our house and I enjoyed it. People who visit zoos enjoy seeing animals, so zoos are good for people. But, now I don't think a zoo is a good place for animals. Imagine you are kept in a cage. You have a place for living and enough food to eat. But you can't get out of the cage all your life. I don't want to live in that situation.

Jack ： I know what you mean. But if you are in the situation all your life, you will think it is comfortable. If everyone around you lives like that, no one thinks it's wrong.

Lisa ： That may be right. But I still don't think animals in cages are happy.

Jack ： Well, then, do you want to see animals in a near-natural environment?

Lisa ： Of course those animals are more interesting, but they are not wild animals.

Jack ： What do you mean?

Lisa ： The environment around the animals is near-natural, but it is not as good as real nature.

Jack ： I see. So don't you think that kind of zoos are good?

Lisa ： I think they are very good for animals. Animals in those zoos are happier than those in cages. But, still they are given food. That means they are not living in the wild. Wild animals have to look for and get food themselves. If they can't, they will die. Animals in zoos are different.

Jack ： OK. I think those zoos are good for small children. Parents take their children to those zoos and the children can see the animals, touch them, give them food, and even take pictures with them. That experience will give children very happy memories and they may always be interested in animals even when they grow up.

Lisa ： I agree.

Jack ： By the way, do you know that animals which are taken care of by people live longer than wild animals?

Lisa ： How much longer do they live?

Jack ： For example, according to a study, a kind of monkeys live only 25 to 30 years in the wild, but they live for about 35 years if they are kept in a zoo. Almost all animals live longer in a zoo than in the wild, and some animals in a zoo live much longer.

Lisa ： That's interesting. Living long is good, but it doesn't always mean being happy.

Jack ： The same thing may be said about people. People say living long is good, but some very old people often say they feel lonely because their family and friends already died.

Lisa ： For animals, that's a difficult question because we cannot understand how they feel.

Question ： What does Lisa think about zoos? Explain her opinions and reasons in English. You have five minutes to write. Now begin.

No.2

Kevin ： Helen, did you read the passage about smartphones?

Helen ： Yes, I did. Kevin, what do you think about smartphones?

Kevin ： In fact, I bought a smartphone a few months ago, and I've found it really useful. When I see people who are using cell phones, not smartphones, on the train, I think why they don't have smartphones. I want to tell them to get smartphones because they are much better.

Helen ： I see. I myself have one, but smartphones are more expensive than other phones. And I think there are a lot of bad points about smartphones. For example, as the passage says, seeing the light from the smartphone for a long time can hurt your eyes. And if you see that light just before you go to bed, maybe you won't be able to sleep well.

Kevin ： That's right. I'm trying to reduce time spent on my smartphone, especially at night. But I often do that.

Helen ： I understand. Time passes really fast when I'm using it. And there's another thing I want to say about smartphones.

Kevin ： What is it?

Helen ： There are a lot of people who are using their smartphones when they are walking on a street or on the platform of a station. It's very dangerous. Once I saw a young woman who was looking at her smartphone on a street. She was crossing the street when the traffic light was red! Luckily, she wasn't hit by a car.

Kevin ： I see those people, too. That's a bad point. It's true that smartphones take a lot of time to study away from us, but we can use smartphones for studying.

Helen ： What do you mean?

Kevin ： Smartphones have not only books and magazines but also lots of dictionaries, so when I do my homework or write a report, I use those dictionaries. They are lighter to carry than paper ones. My parents say they had to carry very heavy books and dictionaries when they were in school.

Helen ： Oh, my parents say the same thing. And another very bad thing is that if you lose your smartphone, it will be a very serious problem. Do you remember the phone numbers of your friends and family members?

Kevin ： No. They are too long to remember. They are all on my smartphone.

Helen ： Almost everyone that has a smartphone is in the same situation. Phone numbers, e-mail addresses, text messages, photos, and other important information are all on the smartphone. We must never lose our smartphones.

Kevin ： I agree.

Helen ： I've said some bad things about smartphones, but I'm sure I'll keep using mine in the future.

Kevin ： Me, too.

Question ： What does Helen think about smartphones? Explain her opinion and reasons in English. You have five minutes to write. Now begin.